HAMMERED BY THE WAVES

A Young Frenchman's Sojourn in Newfoundland in 1882-83

Henri de la Chaume

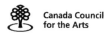 **Canada Council** **Conseil des Arts**
for the Arts **du Canada**

Canadä

 Newfoundland Labrador

We gratefully acknowledge the financial support of the Canada Council for the Arts, the Government of Canada through the Book Publishing Industry Development Program (BPIDP), and the Government of Newfoundland and Labrador through the Department of Tourism, Culture and Recreation for our publishing program.

Cover Design by Todd Manning
Layout by Joanne Snook-Hann
Printed on acid-free paper

Published by
CREATIVE PUBLISHERS
an imprint of CREATIVE BOOK PUBLISHING
a Transcontinental Inc. associated company
P.O. Box 8660, Stn. A
St. John's, Newfoundland and Labrador A1B 3T7

Printed in Canada by:
TRANSCONTINENTAL INC.

Library and Archives Canada Cataloguing in Publication

La Chaume, Henri de
        Hammered by the waves : a young Frenchman's sojourn in Newfoundland in 1882-83 / by Henri de la Chaume ; translated by James M.F. McGrath ; edited with an introduction by Robin McGrath.

Translation of: Terre-Neuve et les Terre-Neuviennes.
Includes bibliographical references.
ISBN 978-1-897174-54-8

        1. La Chaume, Henri de--Travel--Newfoundland and Labrador. 2. Newfoundland and Labrador--Social life and customs. 3. Newfoundland and Labrador--Description and travel. I. McGrath, Robin II. McGrath, James M. F. III. Title.

FC2167.3.L3213 2010   917.1804'2   C2010-901527-4

HAMMERED BY THE WAVES

*A Young Frenchman's Sojourn
in Newfoundland in 1882-83*

Henri de la Chaume

*Translated by Dr. James McGrath
Edited with an Introduction by Robin McGrath*

CREATIVE PUBLISHERS

TABLE OF CONTENTS

Introduction

Terre-Neuve et les Terre-Neuviennes, a translation of which appears here under the title "Hammered by the Waves," was written by Henri de la Chaume and released by the publishing house of Plon Nourrit et cie, Paris, in 1886. De la Chaume, who was just 23 when he wrote *Terre-Neuve et les Terre-Neuviennes*, describes the book as "nothing more than a page in the life abroad of a young Frenchman, artist and poet in his day, as every well-born man ought to be in these times." De la Chaume was being tongue-in-cheek in characterizing his book that way, but it is in many ways an accurate summation of the work. The book provides a vivid portrait of life among the middle classes of St. John's at that time, from the perspective of an enthusiastic and artistic observer.

Terre-Neuve et les Terre-Neuviennes was translated in the winter of 1960-61 by my father, James M.F. McGrath. A medical doctor by training, de la Chaume's was the only work of this sort McGrath ever completed, although before his death in 1975, he had made a start at translating the works of Father Baudoin, the priest who accompanied D'Iberville's expedition against the English in Newfoundland in 1696. Unlike de la Chaume, McGrath had no musical or artistic abilities, but he was something of a poet, and as he occasionally reminded his numerous offspring, he had once been a romantic young man abroad himself. His empathy with young Henri and his intimate knowledge of Newfoundland history, the seal fishery, St. John's society and even the French Shore—McGrath's father had been the Bait Act Commissioner—made him the right man for the job of translating the book.

HENRI DE LA CHAUME

Henri de la Chaume was born on April 14, 1861, at Mayac, Dordogne, France. His mother, Julia Duret de Brie, died when he was very young. His father, Emile de la Chaume, had trained as a lawyer but eventually entered the diplomatic service. When Emile was posted abroad, Henri and his two sisters were left at their father's country estate in Castang near Perigueux.

According to his biographer, Mary M. White, Henri de la Chaume was brought up by German governesses, and later attended boarding school. He did not train for any specific profession, but when he had completed his studies he joined his father who had just been appointed Vice-Consul at St. John's, Newfoundland, as "a commercial or trade attaché." Henri was 20 years old and spoke almost no English at that time, but he possessed "a keen sense of humour and the vivaciousness of youth." In St. John's, he made the acquaintance of a young man who was a French tutor at several local schools and, through him, Henri met a number of young Newfoundlanders who spoke excellent French.

MAYAC, DORDOGNE, birthplace of Henri de la Chaume.

Although Newfoundland was a somewhat hostile environment for Emile de la Chaume, due to the quarreling between French and English fishermen over privileges granted to the French to fish along certain parts of the coast, Henri seems to have found congenial company in the Capital city. He attended parties at Government House, went to Mass regularly at the Roman Catholic Cathedral, attended theatrical performances, and made numerous excursions out into the countryside.

Henri was a gifted artist, and he amused himself with sketching his new friends and the town itself. Two of these sketches have survived, one of Lucretia Stabb[1] and one of St. John's harbour, drawn from the area around Fort William on St. Patrick's Day, 1883.[2]

After 17 months in Newfoundland, Emile de la Chaume complained of ill health and asked for leave from his post. He left the country on October 19th, 1883, for England and then France, and did not return. Henri left the following day, and after taking the opportunity to see a little more of North America, he sailed from New York on November 14th for Le Havre.

Shortly after Henri de la Chaume arrived back in France, he married Jeanne Clarke of Dromantin, a woman of Irish descent, settled into an estate in Cognac and took up horticulture, presumably after completing his book about Newfoundland. The couple had three sons and a daughter, and no doubt Henri felt life had been very kind to him, but here his story takes a very dark turn. Two of his sons were killed outright in the First World War, the third was wounded and died, and in 1918, his wife, "worn out by grief over the loss" died also.

After Jeanne's death, Henri lived at the Abbey of Chancelade, Dordogne, where "he played the organ in the chapel and decorated the nave with his paintings." In 1932, at the age of 71, he moved in with his daughter and her children, his four grandsons and a granddaughter.   The granddaughter, Madame Solange Chavanat, recalled for Miss White that her grandfather "often spoke of the 17 months he had spent in St. John's and retained many happy memories of life there."

Terre-Neuve et les Terre-Neuviennes is a curious little book, because it employs poetic licence to a high degree, while still retaining the respect and even the affection of its readers. There are a number of errors of fact, such as the distance from St. John's to Harbour Grace, but of more significance perhaps are two sections that are clearly fictional.

The first invention is what Albert Perlin refers to as "a long conversation he pretends to have with Sir Edward Shea on the French Shore question." Perlin notes that "It was hardly likely, as de la Chaume asserts, that Shea, then Colonial Secretary, would have listened quietly and silently to a Frenchman who abused hospitality and violated courtesy by pouring invective on the Prime Minister and setting up a powerful rhetorical defence of French fishing rights."[3]

The second major element of fiction is de la Chaume's account of a voyage to the ice to observe the seal fishery. According to Shannon Ryan, the S.S. *French Shore* was a creation of de la Chaume. There were no steamer

ABBEY OF CHANCELADE, DORDOGNE, FRANCE. De la Chaume lived here for many years after the deaths of his wife and sons.

disasters in 1883 or 1884, and the *Greenland*, which really did suffer a disaster in 1898, sailed out of Harbour Grace, not St. John's.[4]

A number of small details confirm that the voyage is not an eyewitness account. "The men did not sleep in the 'forecastle'," Ryan points out, "but in the hold back aft where there was by this time a between deck directly over the main hold and pounds which were filled with coal and this coal was hauled by block and tackle from the hold and passed in baskets by hand to the firemen (a constant nightly activity) and as the coal was burned the pounds were cleaned and the seal pelts stored there—all observers to the seal hunt noted the dirty difficult work of moving the coal."

Other details, such as the equipment used, the methods of killing employed, the food and drink available to the swilers, and so on, are inaccurate, but then as Ryan notes, "Since the *French Shore* is a fictitious ship it experienced a number of fictitious happenings." Despite this, Shannon Ryan admits that "many of Henri's descriptions and comments are fair and he was a good writer. He was certainly recording what he heard as local knowledge in St. John's at the time."

The English translation of de la Chaume's book, published here, came about as a result of the icy St. John's winters Henri so disliked. Premier Joseph Smallwood, an avid collector of Newfoundland and Labrador books, had bought the book in 1960 but did not know French, so he loaned it to McGrath, with the request that he should read it and tell him what it was about. Like many Newfoundlanders, McGrath had studied French at school, but he had also spent his summers in France when he was a medical student in Ireland in the 1920s, and had maintained his fluency by occasionally speaking French to various relatives, but primarily by reading and rereading the classics of French literature.

That winter, while on his way to work, McGrath fell on the ice, shattering his ankle. The fracture demanded bed rest for some time, and it was while he was recovering from this fall that he undertook the translation. As a result of the broken ankle, Mr. Smallwood got not just a summation but the entire book in English. I was 12 years old at the time, and I recall those days quite vividly.

My father lay for weeks surrounded by papers and dictionaries, enthusing over the work, reading bits of it to my mother and endlessly discussing the exact meaning of particular passages. His intention was to achieve not just a literal translation of the words, but to catch the flavour of the book, the enthusiasm and the joy of it. I believe he succeeded in that.

Initially, the translation was typed out on onionskin and hand bound. If I remember correctly, there were six copies in total, one of which went to Mr. Smallwood, one to the archive, one to journalist Albert Perlin (a former colleague), and one which he kept. I do not know where the other two copies landed. Shortly after that, my mother was taken ill and several months later my father had a serious heart attack which greatly curtailed any plans he might have had for publishing the translation.

In a letter to Mr. Smallwood, he wrote that "the faults of the book are obvious. There are many errors of fact and some of the experiences he describes are clearly mythical....But in spite of the faults it is a delightful book. He puts down his impressions with all the directness of a child, sometimes, indeed, of an *enfant terrible*. He is often anything but complimentary in his descriptions, but he shows, behind all the criticism, a real love of Newfoundland and Newfoundlanders and he agrees, with Casanova, that Newfoundland codfish, properly prepared, is one of God's great gifts to the human race."[5]

At the time he did the translation, my father knew nothing of de la Chaume except what the author tells us in his book, but by chance, the work came to the attention of Mary M. White, who taught French at Memorial University and who took a great interest in the history of the French in Newfoundland. Miss White, who came across *Terre-Neuve et les Terre-Neuviennes* in the Archives de la Marine in Paris during the summer of 1968, decided that she would eventually translate the work, and began doing preliminary research on de la Chaume.

How Miss White and McGrath came to realize that they were both interested in the same project I do not know. However, they must have because in September of that year McGrath began making serious enquiries about copyright law with a view to finding a publisher for his translation. Miss White agreed to write the introduction to the work and the following summer she returned to France where she met with de la Chaume's daughter, granddaughter and grandson.

In a letter to McGrath following her visit with the de la Chaume descendents, Miss White wrote "I have waited until now to complete the outline of the introduction to the book as I had various questions to ask the family. I shall begin to do that without delay and shall send it to you. I hope to have the pictures to send along with it."[6] Two photographs of Henri were present in the file with the letters, but there was no introduction.

Why "Newfoundland: The Land and its Ladies" never appeared in print is a mystery. Miss White published an account of her research about Emile and Henri de la Chaume in the *Newfoundland Quarterly*, and a note at the end asserts that "It is hoped that the book—"Newfoundland: The Land and its Ladies"—will be published in English at a later date."[7] The English title indicates that it was McGrath's translation Miss White had in mind. All of the biographical information contained in this Introduction derives from Miss White's article and letters.

It is possible that the early onset of age and ill health on the part of both Miss White and McGrath brought the project to a halt. However, my own feeling is that Henri's life turned out so sadly that my father could no longer bear to think about him. He had so obviously empathized with this young man, who took such delight in exploring Newfoundland, just as my father himself had explored France back in his youth, and for Henri to have lost all three of his sons and his wife was the kind of nightmare that would have haunted his sleep.

The translation presented here is as McGrath left it. I have corrected spelling, capitalization and punctuation, and I have modernized the paragraphing to make the text easier for the general reader (Henri favoured one sentence paragraphs), but otherwise I have changed almost nothing. A little of the syntax has been smoothed out, but clearly McGrath intended to retain the French flavour of de la Chaume's language in his English translation, perhaps to remind readers of the author's Gallic roots. Wherever possible, I have identified people the author identified only by initials, and given explanations for figures who would have been celebrities in their day. Notes that originated with the author and the translator have their initials appended and the rest have been added by the editor.

I would like to thank Joan Ritcey of the Centre for Newfoundland Studies for prompting me to revisit the manuscript; Shannon Ryan for his comments on the sealing section of the book; Larry Dohey of the Archives of the Roman Catholic Archdiocese of St. John's for information on the priests who served in the city in 1882-83; L. Cleary of the Centre for Newfoundland Studies and Aimee Chaulk of Them Days Archives for assistance in obtaining photographs; Gerhard Bassler for information on the German Consul of the day; Elizabeth Yeoman and my sister Antonia McGrath for clarifying the attribution of quotations in the French edition and for assistance in negotiating the original French text; Susan Felsberg for proof-reading and my sister Janet Kelly for permission to publish this work. Above all, I would like to thank Donna Francis and Janine Lilly of Creative Books for taking on an obscure manuscript that has languished far too long in a bottom drawer.

Robin McGrath
Goose Bay, 2010

PART I

The Land and its Discovery

The "First of March 1883." Three years have passed since this date and the letter commenced on that day to a friend of mine is still in my hands, unfinished. It is there, before my eyes, written in English ink on English paper, and I am abruptly led back to old times which will never return. Just think! Since that day, 18 months have passed already, 18 months of my youth vanished so soon. Eighteen months, and my letter isn't finished yet! Life is short after all.

I who indulged in hopes, I who had ambition, I who, contemptuous of vulgar success aspired to a glory attained by great achievements, what can one do if the beautiful years offer no return? Who will give me the time? How can I dare to undertake a long task if I can't finish a letter in 18 months?

The "First of March 1883." Nearly three years gone—Never mind! I'll transcribe here these few neglected phrases. They will serve as the first part of my work, and at the same time they will prove to my friend that I had the good intention of keeping him in touch with my far-off life.

Newfoundland is a rock hammered by the waves,
at the entry of the Gulf of St. Lawrence. This is a
conception derived only from a chart. For me,
I no more get a desolate impression of unending
sea than do the fashionable bathers of the
Norman sea-coast.

1

A LETTER COMMENCED

ST. JOHN'S, NEWFOUNDLAND, MARCH 1ST, 1883

I WRITE you, my dear friend, out of a desire to send you a journal rather than a letter, to better satisfy your curiosity. If I get to the end of my task you can be sure it will not be without heroic efforts; and in return I ask your indulgence towards what you may find wanting in these few pages.

You, the timeless explorer, who have followed all the routes on all the maps published to this day, have not, doubtless, followed the shore-line of America all the way to Labrador, without noticing, lying in a gulf formed by a river, an island with a prodigiously indented coast. Your atlas will tell you more exactly than I can the latitude and longitude which determine the position of this little country, but perhaps I may have to correct the impression you have of its nature.

Newfoundland is a rock hammered by the waves, at the entry of the Gulf of St. Lawrence. This is a conception derived only from a chart. For me, I no more get a desolate impression of unending sea than do the fashionable bathers of the Norman sea-coast.

Three hundred and seventeen miles from south-west to north, 316 from west to east, with a net of railways under construction—what more is needed to call it a continent? I don't insist on this—others may disagree with me—but speaking to Frenchmen, it's my duty to anticipate any false judgments. It is a big country that I am in and a most interesting description I have to offer.

First the coastline; infinitely cut up and split apart. Everywhere the sea bursts on high cliffs which fall sheer into the sea. The cliffs are of schist, limestone and granite and the long patience of the ocean seems to have been wasted on them in vain. Nowhere is there any sign of its destructive force; no sand or shingle beaches. The harbours are formed of pools communicating with the sea as by a breach in a wall, practically never does a hummock disappear beneath the waves and so the movements of the tides are almost imperceptible.

I have told you that numerous bays and coves lace the coastline of the island throughout all its length. The country is almost unknown a stone's throw from the waterline. Very few people have crossed Newfoundland; three or four only.

From hearsay and from my own observations near St. John's, the land is mostly covered with peat-bogs, innumerable forests and rocky mountains. On the west coast, I am told, there are rich deposits of coal, copper, silver and quarries of marble.

There is no road across the Island, but there is reason to believe that, in the near future, railway lines reaching to different coastal points will allow the people of Newfoundland to form a more definite idea of the country they live in. It is said that the interior holds vast stretches of good land and that lovely trees, both spruce and fir, offer a vast field for exploitation.

Of all that, we have here only a very feeble proof. It's a bit hard on the pride and patriotism of Newfoundlanders, but I must say that in the neighbourhood of St. John's the bounty of nature is lamentably lacking.

The woods consist of fir of miserable size except in the depths of a few valleys. As for other trees, there are only birches, and even these only hold their leaves for about three months. To make up for it, the smaller types of growth are very much at home here. They cover the earth with their gracious and delicate little petals, throwing underfoot a carpet of flowers, as if the path they cover led to the home of some good fairy. And it really leads there; each valley, each clearing has its own, which is a pool of limpid and abundant water. At the end of June, on a beautiful sunny day, everything bursts forth at the same time. The white crown of strawberry plants, the timid purple of the violet, the little delicate bells of the whortle-berry, the sad and perfumed waterlily, like a shell of mother of pearl, and a thousand other flowers coloured from dawn to noonday, whose names are unknown.

But, alas, there should be a butterfly for every flower, a bird for every bush. Here the fauna is a contradiction to the flora. Insects are unhappily represented by mosquitoes. Blackbirds with red bellies here take the place of sparrows. The swallows don't come at all!

In contrast, furred and feathered game are masters of the scene, although they are already scarce near St. John's. Snipe are numerous in this half-submerged land. The partridge, with his plumed feet, becomes white in winter, and ducks of all kinds are, as everywhere, the conscript forerunners of the winter season. In the thickets, the rime-powdered rabbits nibble the mosses under the snow. The Arctic hare, the caribou, the silver fox, the bear, the otter, and other fur-bearing animals, live in the woods of the interior. You will note that, unlike the vegetation, it is the small varieties that are in the minority.

As for the Newfoundland dog, I prefer to say nothing as up to now I strongly doubt his existence. We have a very young sample and we will see what he turns into; but in the nine months that I have been here I haven't yet found one that met my expectations.

Nine months! Yes, nine months, nearly a year since, for the first time, I came ashore on the other side of the ocean. In the month of May I said goodbye to you in the shadows of the park, and I arrived on June first in a country where winter, having gobbled up the spring, had hardly started to give way before summer.

During the last days of the crossing there was an icy blast on the sea, long wet banks of fog swept from one horizon to the other. This produced a strange optical illusion which made the waves seem high as mountains. It was like a vision of infinity.

However, on the morning of our arrival, the sky was clear. Soon we met icebergs that the current was leading south. In the distance, the bluish cliffs of Newfoundland rose before us. I was on the bridge near the Captain—one could almost think that the vessel was stopped and that it was the island that was approaching us. The cloudy outlines became clearer. The waves, the earth and the sky ceased to be confused together in one blue background. Soon the coastal rocks could be seen in clear detail, darker against the paler skies. The ocean, almost black, was surrounded with metallic sparkles, the mountains of ice slashed here and there with fissures of gorgeous emerald. One of the most enormous floated in the narrow gut which gives access to the port of St. John's. As we passed in, a pan of ice split off from its side and the crash of its fall had a reverberation much more formidable than the voice of our guns signaling our entrance to the port.

At that moment, the narrow slit that we had seen between two high walls of rock suddenly enlarged and we entered a harbour whose quiet surface seemed like the arena of an immense amphitheatre. To left and right were sculptured hills with no sign of verdure. They came together at a distance of several miles, to choke the picturesque course of a little stream losing its waters in the bottom of the anchorage. But we could not see it. All we could see were the dark clusters of fir-trees sweeping down the valley, a forest of masts, war ships and fishing boats filled up the foreground.

But it was not to this that our glance was first directed, rather it was to the charming picture presented by this town whose nearest buildings dipped their feet, so to speak, in the sea while the others, rank above rank, climbed to the top of the hill and seemed to crowd around the Catholic cathedral which was lifting its imposing towers to the sky.

SKETCH OF ST. JOHN'S, MARCH 17, 1882. By Henri de la Chaume.

Happy those who stopped at this point and who, without leaving the bridge of the ship, have kept the impression of so smiling a scene. I, who have seen it too closely, shall doubtless only recapture my admiration on the day when leaving these shores. The vessel that shall carry me will allow me to contemplate it again for a last time while saying goodbye.

It was, then, the first of June. This date will certainly arouse in you sensations entirely different to those felt here at the same time. A word, by the way, if you will allow, on the climate and the seasons.

While the ice had left the rivers, the snow on the ground had forgotten to melt in many places. Nature seemed to have no inclination to wake up. Nonetheless the sun began to warm up the earth which was moist from the melting snows. A sort of lukewarm mist seemed to float invisibly in the atmosphere. Next day there was no sun, nothing but cold winter overcoats and the buds cowering in their coverings.

Towards June 15th, the better sheltered ones risked showing their noses. Then, encouraged by a few days' sun, all of a sudden they bloomed *en masse* and by June 30th everything was flowers and leaves. It was summer, brusquely succeeding winter, but a deceptive summer, with burning sunrays and glacial shadows. Once the sun was hidden and the wind blew, one had to muffle up.

"Patience," they said to us. "Patience; we'll soon have Indian Summer. You'll see how beautiful it is." October arrived. The rains stopped. Every morning the sun rose from the waves shining and glowing like gold. It was Autumn. It was Indian Summer and it lasted for nearly two months from mid-September to mid-November.

Then the cold came, little by little, although it is only at New Year that winter discloses all its rigour. The wind, which here has eternal empire, brought it suddenly one day, all clothed with snow.

I must tell you that Newfoundland is the native country of the wind. Certainly Old Aeolus must have a castle here some place. He is always whistling somewhere and bringing notice of tremendous snows to come. But the wind becomes dangerous when it raises great billows of snow so fine and crystallized that it looks like diamond-dust. In a moment one is blinded and powdered from head to foot and one is lucky if one doesn't have to fight the storm to keep one's feet at the same time. Such an adventure happened to me, for the first time, one evening last week. Thank God there were three of us to help each other out.

One curious thing is that the snow here rarely falls in big flakes. I've been told it is the same in the Arctic regions.

From time to time the north wind swings south. The clouds leave the sun free in the sky, and then it is like a mirage of spring with the pale blue sky, the ocean silvered with ice, and the high cliffs sleeping under their blanket of snow. But suddenly the wind is brutally unchained and sweeps along, shivering from the caress of the snow.

One notices that the thermometer registers 20° below zero and that the harbour and the sea are frozen. Then a cannon-shot is heard. It's the steamer bringing the mail from Europe. How will it manage to get to the wharf through a crust of ice a foot and a half thick?

The sight is worth seeing and indeed worth telling. A breach must be made; to do this, the ship rushes full speed ahead at the obstacle like a battering-ram attacking a tower. It forces itself in for about its own length, and since the resistance is too strong, it must make another dash. It goes astern and again thrusts forward with all its force and speed. This attack lasts a longer or shorter period according to the distance from the boat to the wharf. You may figure that it takes about an hour to cover a distance of a mile. You can easily imagine that this kind of navigation, which recalls Don Quixote's tilting with the windmills, demands steamers of special construction and proof against every strain, so the fore plates are as solid as walls.

When a steamboat comes into the anchorage under these conditions, it is highly picturesque. A curious crowd gathers about the steamer or runs before it as it penetrates the ice. Poor old St. Peter would have been very much ashamed of his fear if he saw all the youngsters running around on the waves.

I just told you that the thermometer was down to 20° below zero, which is -29° centigrade. This only happened once, towards the end of January, and I should add that the inhabitants spoke of it only with consternation as of something that had never happened before. Actually, the Newfoundland winter is to be feared more for its duration than its fierceness. One must expect seven months of snow, from October to May. And what snow! It accumulates yards high in many places, so much so that the roads become unusable even for sledges. And as the weather is often clear in the cold season, the sun melts the snow on the surface during the day. As soon as daylight fades, the ice reforms, and as all the streets of the town are more or less on a slope, it becomes impossible to keep upright on this icy surface without ice-creepers on.

April brings the thaw which lasts until the end of May. Often during the night there is a sudden drop in temperature. Next day, everything is sheathed in ice as in enamel. Every object in its smallest details seems encased in a coating of crystal. There is no sight so lovely as a sunbeam giving its burst of light to a clump of trees so transformed. Then one has to flounder around in cold and dirty water for the two most lovely months of April and May. No sign of greenery shows itself before the sudden and definitive appearance of summer. Sometimes, in March, one is tempted to believe that winter is getting ready to depart; but to take away any illusion in this regard, somebody one day quoted to me the old proverb, "When March comes in like a dove it goes out like a lion."

A sad country, isn't it, of which one can say that the year has lost its spring. And is the summer itself much better? June and July are almost always foggy. Sometimes during these two months, one may go 15 days without seeing the sea or the harbour which thick fog completely conceals. Strange to say this fog tends to end along the line of the wharves without coming into the town, so that instead of the harbour with its ships and cliffs, one sees piled up before one a high white wall, opaque and impenetrable. At other times these banks of cloud land in the entrance of the port without coming into the harbour. At such a time it is most interesting to see a vessel come in. When one least expects it, one suddenly sees it emerging into the light like an apparition. In short, one finishes by feeling one is in prison. One has attacks of melancholy. This white wall weighs on the heart and makes the spirit droop. One misses the winter with its limpid skies and above all one longs for Indian Summer.

Let's talk a little of St. John's. First, remember that I live in a town built entirely of wood. Nevertheless, it's the capital of the Island of Newfoundland which calls itself with typical British pride "England's Oldest Colony."

2

ENGLAND'S OLDEST COLONY

I HAVE just made you pass a full year with me. It's putting a strain on your time and friendship, isn't it! But you see my little trick. I know you are very curious so I've saved the best part for the finish and you'll have to listen to me to the end to be satisfied. Did I say "to the end"? My dear friend, there's a good chance I may fall by the wayside.

Let's talk a little of St. John's. First, remember that I live in a town built entirely of wood. Nevertheless, it's the capital of the Island of Newfoundland which calls itself with typical British pride "England's Oldest Colony."

It was the 24th of June, 1497. The fogs are almost continual at this time of the year around Newfoundland, but sometimes a ray of sunlight makes a sudden gash in the fog and it was so on that day when the Virgin Island, bereft of its veil of mist, was surveyed for the first time by the gaze of Europeans.

In a triumphant voice, the lookout who watched from the mizzen-mast of the *Matthew*, a little ship from Bristol, cried out "Land! Land!" The Captain was John Cabot and his son Sebastian was first officer. Cries of delight rose from the poop and the rocks of the shore repeated the astonished echo without understanding these sounds they had never heard before.

History tells us that the codfish took no notice, being unable to guess what miseries were in store for their species, and for which the coming of these men was the signal. At that time they shared with the seals the absolute sovereignty of the Island and its dependencies; but England was not slow to depose them (to its profit) on the ground that Sebastian Cabot, who commanded the *Matthew*, was born in Bristol.

In February of the following year, King Henry VII granted to John Cabot a new Charter authorizing him to undertake another expedition with six ships, but this time the old Italian did not go himself and trusted the mission to his son Sebastian, then 23 years old. Nevertheless, in spite of her evil joy in harpooning each new victim, it was not until 86 years later that Albion sought to establish official power over Newfoundland. In fact, no attempt at colonization was made during this lapse of time of nearly a century.

The seals, already well-known for their diplomatic ability, had arranged for a formal meeting with the codfish. Plenipotentiaries had been named and a conference had assembled on the Grand Banks, which had decided that the utmost prudence must be observed to avoid awakening the *devouring* greed of the English. For this, it was essential to preserve a complete silence and allow no public gatherings.

But 86 years later, the congress having re-assembled to vote felicitations to its members, the English surprised them in the midst of their deliberations and resolved on a general extermination. On that day, four English war-ships and 36 fishing boats of various nationalities found themselves assembled in the port of St. John's.

Sir Humphrey Gilbert landed. Hostages from the seals and codfish were led behind him in chains. Round him, his officers and a crowd of others formed a circle. Sir Humphrey then read a royal proclamation, empowering him to take possession of Newfoundland in the name of Queen Elizabeth and to exercise her jurisdiction in the Island and all other Royal lands in the same region.

Then, turning to the hostages, he told them that their autopsy had been ordered. Two surgeons of the Royal Navy came forward, scalpel in hand, and it was on this occasion that vivisection was carried out for the first time. From the anatomical

SIR HUMPHREY GILBERT. "Hostages from the seals and codfish were led behind him in chains. Round him, his officers and a crowd of others formed a circle."

structure of the cod, it was deduced that its flesh would provide a food both substantial and delicate. As for the seal, its white pelt, thick with fat, promised to make it a precious factor in the industrial development of the country. In consequence, open war was declared against the underwater population and every means was proclaimed fair and proper to gather them in.

The jurisdiction of Sir Humphrey Gilbert, according to the proclamation, extended for 200 leagues in all directions thus taking in, with Newfoundland, Nova Scotia, New Brunswick, a part of Labrador and Prince Edward Island.

It was almost a kingdom and Sir Humphrey had brought with him from Devonshire 250 colonists to begin its settlement. He was supported in his enterprise by his celebrated half-brother, Sir Walter Raleigh. The latter had at first formed part of the expedition led by Sir Humphrey, but disease had broken out on his ship and he had to go back to England. It was thus that the first foundations of England's colonial empire in North America were laid.

But we are concerned with Newfoundland only for the time being, and as its history has little interest, I will only trace for you its main outlines. However, it's worthwhile recalling that the French were the real colonizers of Newfoundland. After the discovery by Cabot, it was the French seaman Cartier, and later Champlain, who came to land on its shores. In 1525, Francis I sent Vevagine in the *Salamander* to explore the newly discovered lands and to announce to the seals and cod that they had passed under his Royal Authority. In 1604 the first French settlement was made and Newfoundland and Acadia (now Nova Scotia) were ours during all of the 17th century and up to the Treaty of Utrecht.

A coalition of our enemies took these lands from us and delivered them up to England. In this period all the fortified places in Newfoundland, and especially St. John's, changed hands a score of times. The year 1713 saw us finally expelled from our ancient possessions, leaving us only the islands of St. Pierre and Miquelon and some fishery rights on part of the Newfoundland coast. These rights, which were afterwards renewed by several treaties, deserve a special study which I will take up later.

What points are left for me to outline to finish this rapid sketch of Newfoundland history? Since these troubled wartimes, nothing could be more peaceable than the establishment and development of the English colonies. In 1855, Newfoundland became an independent Colony. The Island is no longer garrisoned and in St. John's (the capital) the only force at the disposal of the executive power is 50 policemen, about half of them mounted. This is the present state of the country where I am your guide and mentor.

As to the resistance that the Indians have been able to put up against the invasion of their island, one scarcely hears of it. All that is left today of the first masters of Newfoundland are about a half-score families of the Mic-Mac tribe. They are grouped together in a village on the Northern Coast. Inoffensive, and peacefully inclined, they fish in the summer and in winter trap the fur-bearing animals along the rivers and in the little known interior of the island. Isn't it astonishing that a race "sprung from the soil" should have disappeared so quickly in a land still unexplored and about which even opinion is still based on guesswork?

I have told you that only the shoreline is well-known and all the European establishments are by the seashore. Indeed, what is surprising in that? What is the lure that brought and kept here the people of Newfoundland? Fish, and fish only. It is to the seal and the cod that this country owes its colonization. Without these storehouses of treasure for industrial exploitation, this poor dowerless island would still be a desert.

THREE MI'KMAW WOMEN IN BAY ST. GEORGE, photographed by Paul-Émile Miot, a French Naval officer who was surveying the French Shore from the naval vessel *Sésostris* in 1859. "Isn't it astonishing that a race 'sprung from the soil' should have disappeared so quickly?"

All the towns and all the villages have the same origins if not the same founders. The sailors came, first French and then English, looking for a bay or a cove that would give both safe shelter for their boats and wood for the building of cabins and the flakes for the drying of fish. The coast became better known. They learned the places where fish tended to be most plentiful. Fishermen tended to assemble at these points. Some stayed over the winter and started trading on their own; but they were consumers and the country produced nothing. Imports had to balance exports between Newfoundland and Europe; side by side with the fishing rooms rose greater structures, houses and stores. The foundations of a new nation were laid.

At the present time, the total population of the Island is about 180,000, mostly Irish or Scottish. Of these about 30,000 are in St. John's. There are six or seven thousand at Harbour Grace and Twillingate, which, after the capital, are the two most important centres of commerce. I will limit myself to describing St. John's. It's the most interesting town and, besides, it's the only one I know.

Let's go ashore then, if you will,
and go up to make a tour of the town.

3

A Tour of St. John's

DURING the French occupation it was Placentia on the south coast that was the capital of Newfoundland; and it is doubtless due to its superior situation that St. John's dethroned its predecessor. The town was built on the southeast coast on the Avalon Peninsula at the nearest point to Europe.

I have already described its appearance and you know also that it has a deep natural harbour sheltered from all the winds that blow. "The Narrows" at the entrance are only about 600 feet wide. The Harbour is about a mile and a quarter in length and half a mile in width. In the middle it is 90 feet deep. All around, hills from 200 to 600 feet high allow it to sleep quietly, even if a tempest is raging outside. Ships of any tonnage can moor at any time alongside its hospitable wharves.

Let's go ashore then, if you will, and go up to make a tour of the town.

These ruins of walls and fortifications that you see at the harbour-mouth are of French construction. It was indeed our compatriots who started this town which today is entirely English, or rather Newfoundlandish; and if there are no more numerous traces of French origin, it is because of the famous fire which, about 40 years ago, completely swallowed up St. John's. This shocking event has never left the memories of those who saw it, nor of their descendants.

Four or five months ago some Lazarist Missionaries came to give a retreat at the Cathedral. On this occasion a poor man came to the confessional. "How long since your last confession?" asked the priest. "Not since the fire." "What fire?" "The Great Fire." "How long ago was that?" "Oh, about 35 or 40 years!" Among St. John's people "The Great Fire" is like the beginning of Newfoundland history!

After this disaster a law was passed by the House of Assembly ordering that the principal streets must be 50 feet wide and that houses be built of brick. The main commercial street of the town, that runs along the water-front, was actually rebuilt thus, but the rest of the houses are of wood.

But that would not affect the appearance nor the charm of the town, were it not that in other ways there is much to criticize. In summer the slightest fall of rain turns the street into a morass and the slightest breeze with a gleam of sun raises billows of dust in a moment. Paving is a thing absolutely unknown. It's worse if you seek refuge on the sidewalks. Then look out! They are made of planks laid side by side; three quarters of them rotted away. Nothing is so dangerous for a stranger than to risk going out at night. In the absence of a moon the town is scarcely lighted at all, and you never know when you may put your foot in a hole or knock against some unseen obstacle.

In winter the streets are never cleared and according to the caprice of the weather, one must, if one goes out, resign oneself either to getting stuck in the snow or trying to stand up on a surface armoured in ice. Do you know the Alps? Think of a town built on a glacier.

All that comes from having no Municipal Council, and the absence of a governing body comes from lack of money, and the lack of money is because the townsmen don't want to pay taxes. A water tax is the only one the government has succeeded in imposing. But in this matter one must agree that it is everything one might wish for. The water runs day and night in the houses and through the town and gives a strong promise of cleanliness.

What shall I tell you of the external appearance of the town? Its few monuments are not very distinguished! The most venerable, both by its site and proportions and its richness, is the Catholic Cathedral, which is of no very definite style, although all its openings are full arches. The Anglican Cathedral, of which a part is still under construction, will be no less vast than the other; but in spite of its Gothic windows, it will always be outclassed by its rival whose imposing towers rise skyward on the high point of the hill.

The House of Assembly is a great cut-stone structure with a Greek facade. Government House, residence of the Governor, is nothing more or less than a huge barracks made up of a main building flanked on right and left by wings with neither dignity nor style. What else? The fine College of St. Patrick directed by the priests. The Atheneum Hall with its fine concert and lecture rooms. The rest are not worth mentioning.

You are probably waiting for me to tell you about the lovely walks along the seashore and the wharves! But, my dear friend, you are forgetting that everything here is for codfish, not for men. The road nearest the harbour runs along with scarcely a sight of it except for a few glimpses. The row of houses and shops of traders separates one from it. Every merchant has, behind his house, his store and his wharf built of wood on piles which gain access to the street by a passage under the house.

Now that I've taken you through all the streets of the town, let me hope, my poor friend, that I haven't bored you too much. Come and let me show you the interior of the places I have led you to and let me tell you what goes on in them…

GOVERNMENT HOUSE, ST. JOHN'S, 1851. "Government House…is nothing more or less than a huge barracks made up of a main building flanked on right and left by wings with neither dignity nor style."

There, then, with a few modifications, is the letter I commenced on March 1st, 1883. As I feared, I never finished it. Today I take it back to address it to the great public. Will I keep my promises any better to them? I don't know! Let me keep trying, anyhow, and let me hope that my efforts, if they succeed, will merit from them encouragement for the future.

PART II

Society and Local Life

During the last months of my stay in Newfoundland, bored by the monotony of my existence, I was guilty of keeping a sort of journal. Many of the pages were written with a quill plucked from the wing of the blue-bird of memory. Others were sketched from real life mixed with observations and stories that at least have the merit of truth. By selecting from all this I hope to interest the reader by disclosing to him the character of the St. John's people and their manner of living.

To those who expect to open a book of profound and solemn studies, it may be as well to say that I was 20 years old when I landed on the shores of America, and at the time I am writing I have not enough of a mustache to inspire any respectful fear in the charming children who call me uncle. This is, then, nothing more than a page in the life abroad of a young Frenchman, artist and poet in his day, as every well-born man ought to be in these times. Even if I mix into my story a few flights of poetry, will not this serve to render it more real and truthful? Is not there more of dreaming and loving in life than in a romance? And can I help it if the women there are far superior to the men and almost obliged me to spend most of my time in the study of their sex?

I knew already, and it was one of the first things I learned on landing, that there were lots of pretty faces in the town. "The girls here are charming" they told me. "You are going to be entertained and welcomed most warmly by them."

1

A Ball, a Visit and a Bouquet

TWO days after my arrival in Newfoundland, I entered flat-footed into St. John's society. There was a ball at Government House. I found myself with official standing and I was invited. What would this affair be like? I knew already, and it was one of the first things I learned on landing, that there were lots of pretty faces in the town. "The girls here are charming" they told me. "You are going to be entertained and welcomed most warmly by them."

We made our way through the curious crowd on the Allan Company's wharf. At our passage, eyes sparkled and ears alerted without understanding anything. Behind us, Russian, German and Irish emigrants, coming off the wharf, filled the gangway with their swarming misery. Then the blocks shrieked, the hoists went to work in the ship's bowels and slowly and painfully, one by one, they lifted heavy bales which they let go only to fasten on another prey. In little groups, the ship's company and the townsmen left the wharf. At the foot of a wall a crowd had assembled.

"What's that?"

"Nothing–only two sailors altering each other's faces with their fists!"

I was satisfied that it was just local colour! Besides, the sky was blue. The sun was almost warm. I was alive, after 10 days of discomfort on a cold sea.

That evening, from far-off one could still hear the shrill scream of the winch, relentless at its task of unloading the steamer. It shrilled out sudden as a thunderclap and then would stop as suddenly. The work was carried on by the red light of flares. I had to go down there as a bag was missing from my luggage. A narrow ladder which plunged down into the darkness brought me to the bottom of the ship's hold. I stumbled on the hummocky surface of all kinds of bales, knocking my head against the partitions and often obliged to wriggle backwards without room to turn around. Lord, how brilliant the stars seemed and how bright even the shadows were when, stretched out straight on the little ladder, my elbows at my side and my head high, I felt the clear air about me.

No less agreeable was the sensation I felt a few evenings later when I made my first visit to the impressive drawing rooms of the administrator. I was far from imagining, when I left Paris, that I would find in Newfoundland a real society, or even anything approaching what we call society.

"Do you know St. John's in Newfoundland?"

"Surely, that's where they dry codfish."

"So you think. Follow me for a moment."

There is no governor at the moment, but a simple administrator who represents him. His Honour Sir F.B.T.C., K.C.M.G.[8] I am presented, but I only know as yet three words in English, and even these don't go together, and he is not much better in French. Happily, an Englishman can put into a handshake all that he thinks but can't express. So this time our conversation was limited to this act of courtesy.

The administrator might not be a great man, but he is a big man. He comes towards you, always affable, his hand held out, his little eyes twinkling in a face like that of an elderly baby. Seeing you from a distance he hastens, to do you honour, to take off his right glove, so as to give you his bare hand to clasp. Every proper gentleman does that in these parts. He is very proud of his Grand Cross and red ribbon, is the administrator. There are three or four like him in Newfoundland whom the Queen has distinguished with the insignia of "Knight Companion of St. Michael and St. George" which they always indicate with the greatest

SIR FREDERICK BOWKER TERRINGTON CARTER. "The administrator might not be a great man, but he is a big man."

care after their names by the initials K.C.M.G. This Order, created for the colonies and only there really honoured, gives to its holder the right to the title "Sir."

It's hard to believe how much this little word can fill the mouth of an Englishman. In Newfoundland, the most insignificant politician who has the good fortune to be able to call himself "Sir" is at that moment ordained a great man. What is even more delightful is that he himself believes it even though he is only "Sir" by virtue of his K.C.M.G., and he has soon had his ancestry traced back to William the Conqueror. In fact, as usually nobody knows where he comes from, he is free to say what he likes. Prouder than an English Duke, he lords it over everyone around him and, to the stranger who ventures to smile, everyone says "But he's a *Sir*, don't you realize that, he's a *Sir!*"

Ah, Madame, what a lovely dress that is, swishing against my legs! They tell me it's from Paris and that could well be. It's of cloud-coloured silk, wonderfully set off with rows of pearls. But somehow this dress—I'm told now that it's from Worth's—is not perfect, something is lacking. It has no chic. Wait a moment—the dress has chic—it's the girl who lacks it.

I ask the Secretary "Who is that ravishing creature who has just come in?"

"Where do you see her?"

"There—that brunette who is wearing a dress of shot-silk embroidered with pearls like a Parisienne, with a bunch of red roses in her corsage."

"Oh—that's my daughter."

Happy father. He has four like that, each more accomplished than the other, and all speaking French.

I had hardly time to be presented to this young queen, when a dancer snatched her away. But soon I was introduced to another French-speaking young lady.

"Mademoiselle, will you give me the honour of this dance?

"Certainly, sir, unless you prefer to chat."

I hasten to accept, and soon, taking my arm, she led me out of the drawing room and we sauntered in a large corridor where other couples were already strolling. I was astonished by this freedom of manners which I found adorable. Papa and Mama didn't question it. What had they to do with us? They weren't even pointed out to me—and anyway neither of them knew a word of French. Miss Esther, on the contrary, spoke it very well with just a touch of English accent to remind one of her nationality.

In a moment, more strollers flowed into the corridor through all the doors. Here, instead of gravely leading one's dancing-partner to the shelter of the maternal wing, when one has ceased to whirl around, one offers her one's arm until the next dance, one strolls and chats and in a word, one flirts.

At the first note of the orchestra, I thought—I was stuffed with misconceptions— that convention and discretion made it my duty to bring Miss Esther back to her place.

"You're going to dance?" she asked me.

"I have no intention of it."

"Then let's keep chatting. It's much more fun."

That was my opinion too. I had never been at such a party and I savoured with delight the honey of flirtation as a Frenchman would who had never before enjoyed this delicacy, and the conversation took its course, touching on everything, without embarrassment or impediment. The last waltz began, Miss Esther had promised it and, withdrawing her arm from mine, which she had been holding for more than an hour, she told me she was counting on a visit from me on the following day.

Today is Sunday and the day has commenced by bringing me several more causes for astonishment. First of all, eleven o'clock Mass at the Cathedral. The first Sunday the Colonial Secretary had kindly admitted me to his pew. I could not do less, in face of such a courteous gesture, than to follow the example of my neighbours, so that, coming out of the church at noon I couldn't help feeling my poor knees practically stiffened by the hard usage I'd given them.

This morning, thanks to Miss Esther, I was in the organ-loft. I met there a dozen young girls of the best families who came there every Sunday to sing in the choir. Be sure that the first rule they made was that each could have a young man to escort her. Behold me then, introduced into this choir of virgins and seated next to my protectress and, to myself, having the air of a wolf in a sheepfold. I quickly got used to the situation and I even believe that the Mass seemed shorter than the first time. It's true that my ears were charmed beyond expression.

Suddenly a fine, fresh voice, delightfully silver-toned and managed with consummate art, breathed the first strains of Mercadante's "Ave Maria." At the end of the piece I was in heaven. It would be impossible to breathe these long phrases with a more harmonious sweetness. Impossible to instill more soul into the ardour of the invocation. How that voice imperceptibly faded away, high and far. How it came back in warm deep-toned passion. I was in an ecstasy, invoking in turn the names of Van Zandt and of Patti, and told myself that if my soul could be intoxicated often with this voice, that I would be happy enough in Newfoundland.

When she had finished, Miss Fisher modestly resumed her place by the organ. As soon as possible, I had myself presented to her to offer her the homage of my admiration.[9] I was stupefied to learn that she was an actress and a Protestant! She came there not only with the consent, but at the request of the Bishop. After a time he persuaded her to come every Sunday. Eighteen months later, about the time of my departure, her talent had reached such a point that, hearing Patti in New York, I said to myself I couldn't believe that Miss Fisher could have sung so well. It seems she was in St. John's by chance, caring for her mother who was very ill for a long time.

Other surprises were to come to me that same day. As we came down from the organ-loft the Abbe Galveston,[10] an artist

MISS CLARA FISHER. "I was stupefied to learn that she was an actress and a Protestant!"

and already a friend, passed me on the stairs and stopped to speak with a young girl. I had not yet met her and, as I was passing, she had herself introduced to me by the priest. I shook Miss Lizzie's hand and continued to follow Miss Esther. Two of her friends, who seemed to be watching us, stopped under the porch to ask similarly for an introduction. I was confused, almost bewildered by the careless boldness with which these young girls threw themselves at young men. The last two, Catherine, whom they called Kitty, and her sister Bessie, spoke French as well as I did.

I went on with Miss Esther who waited nearby and whom I escorted home. It was on this occasion I first met her parents. In a moment, port and sherry were brought in. It is the custom of the country to serve these wines to visitors. The climate allows some freedom in the use of alcoholic liquors. In winter it is even necessary to take them and in the evenings they like to warm the blood with a big glass of hot whisky and water.

When he had drunk his sherry, Miss Esther's father, knowing quite well that it was not he I had come to see, discreetly retired and left me alone with his daughter. After a sustained conversation and a few moments at the piano, I took my leave and was invited to come often and pass an evening.

On the walk back I mused on the surprising liberty given to these young girls; at the free permission given them to meet young men; to

MICHAEL FRANCIS HOWLEY. "As we came down from the organ loft the 'Abbe Galveston', an artist and already a friend, passed me on the stairs."

receive them alone, in the evening as well as the day, without the parents being previously consulted as to selecting the young men introduced into the household. I admired this absolute confidence on the part of the father and mother, a confidence well-merited you can be sure, as it was never abused. How far I was from France! What a difference in customs and mode of living! And how this frequent and intimate association with young girls served to fill a man's heart with a tender respect and an affectionate esteem for womanhood.

I had reached that point in my reverie when a light English wagon which was coming towards me suddenly stopped nearby. I had barely time to recognize Miss Lizzie and raise my hat to her. "Climb up next to me. I am bringing you to the house," she said to me in her own pleasant style of French. I thought at first I must have misunderstood or that she herself didn't quite understand the meaning of the words she used. I tried to excuse myself, but she insisted and taking my courage in my hands I perched myself beside her. I asked myself in terror what degree of scandal we were going to create along the streets, for she lived out of town, almost in the country, and we had to drive all through St. John's.

I knew that there were about four women here for every man, and in consequence the young girls had great difficulty in getting engaged and were said to be man-chasers. Here the struggle for life gives way to the struggle for a wedding. I thought myself already compromised, obliged to appear before the Consul who, exercising both his official and paternal authority, would doubtless have given me a very poor reception, not finding the union to his taste. I didn't feel myself much inclined to marriage—especially this marriage. However, seeing that the passers-by paid no particular attention to us, I began to calm down bit by bit.

Miss Lizzy spoke very little French, but made up in quantity what was lacking in quality. I helped her out when a word would not come and finished for her phrases that she would start. "You French folk are very kind" she said. "You never make fun of people who speak your language badly and you help them to express themselves in French. The English, on the contrary, laugh at

CARICATURE OF TOM 'MARA
by Michael Francis Howley.

the slightest fault, and never whisper a word to help out a difficulty."

Soon we arrived at Flower Hill. All the family were drawn up to receive us, but Lizzie is almost the only one I can understand, so the drawing room seemed like a marionette theatre. As I had drunk port at Esther's, I chose to drink sherry here. To escape a second glass that the father urged upon me, I bowed and took my way to the door. Miss Lizzie came with me as far as the garden gate and along the way plucked a bouquet that she offered me as I left. "Wait a moment," she said, "I'm going to put them in your buttonhole." At that moment I vowed to myself that I would never again be surprised at anything from a young Anglo-American girl.

November—How strange that I haven't so far spoken of Benoit, my only countryman. I hear him coming in and that awakes my memory. Benoit, the man for every moment, for every usefulness, for every service, for all information and for all good nature. Knowing him one can hardly help thinking, on seeing him, of what Choufleurt said of his servant. "Lord, Lord, how stupid he is—but how devoted!!!"

Our good Benoit, like the Norman that he is, is a little foolish. More often than the average, he tends to put his foot in it. But he's so obliging, he has such a strong character and he takes rebuffs with so much philosophy! All his qualities can be read in his jolly round face, a bit high-coloured, with a fleshy nose planted right in the middle, but the tip of which juts out with an invincible prejudice against the straight lines. In this it follows the example of his mustache, coarse haired and stiff, yellow-brown in colour and apparently always blown to one side by an invisible wind.

Prosper Benoit is the only Frenchman in St. John's. Having done badly in business in our near-by colony of St. Pierre-Miquelon, he came here to try his fortune again. He speaks English almost as badly as the French which he teaches in several colleges and to many individuals in the town. It's his daily bread and the poor man has no other means to support his family than by following this occupation, which in all weathers, through ice and snow, forces him to give private lessons from morn 'til night. He has been of the greatest help to me since my arrival here, since I could speak no English. How much information has he given me. How many messages and commissions has he carried out, in how many places has he been my interpreter; and all that in the most distinguished fashion, in a fine spirit of patriotism.

In no part of the world are clergy so tolerant. They could scarcely be otherwise if a good understanding is to be maintained in a population half Catholic and half Protestant.

2

The Colonial Clergy

DECEMBER 26th—Yesterday was Christmas and a radiantly sunny day. I dined with the Bishop—that is I passed part of the day with him and I seize this occasion to talk of him and of his works and his clergy.[11]

The Catholic Cathedral is built on a marvellous site. It can be seen from everywhere in the town and dominates every vista. From there the view disappears in a distance that cannot be taken in by the eye. Between two tumbling hills, one can glimpse the sea, which seems to flow out of the harbour and mingle its spreading waves of aqua-marine with the sky. If some ship leaves the port and sails towards Europe, one sees her for hours, steaming straight ahead, getting smaller and smaller until she disappears in a fold of invisible

CATHEDRAL OF ST. JOHN THE BAPTIST, 1878. "The Catholic Cathedral is built on a marvelous site. It can be seen from everywhere in the town and dominates every vista."

vapour. If she is sailing coast-wise, she is visible only for a moment as she swings around the cliffs. One by one, her masts disappear behind the rocks while the ensign flying at the peak of her mizzen vanishes in a last goodbye. Suddenly the sea is empty, sinister as a closing tomb. Infinity seems to close in on it until a scarcely perceptible sail brings life back on its white wing.

The sea is sad seen from on high. It lifts its mass to the mid-sky and the strongest surges scarcely cause a ripple on it. Before this menacing calm, meditation should be easier and more consoling for a priest, and if this is so, the Bishop of St. John's is well situated to have his prayers mount heavenward. The Episcopal Palace is right next to the Cathedral.

BISHOP THOMAS JOSEPH POWER.
"He is truly a prince of the church. He reigns as father and orders as a king among his subjects."

The Bishop is a charming man, young, active and intelligent, and all these qualities easily find employment for his is an imposing position. More than half the residents of St. John's, over 15,000 souls, are his faithful and obedient subjects. He is truly a prince of the church. He reigns as father and orders as a king among his subjects. Far from abusing his power, he uses it only with the most scrupulous moderation and never in his own private interest. It's true that he would be hard put to it to express any deficiency, for he does the honours of his establishment with a satisfaction that lights up his countenance. He shows you his stables, his kitchen garden, his orchard, his poultry yard, not in vanity, but because he enjoys it all and wants you to enjoy it too. For the rest he is a lover of moderation and an admirer of La Belle France. He understands French with difficulty, but in spite of that can use it for little jokes that he loves to make.

His weakness is a deplorable nervousness. From the moment he is in company, he is in a state of nerves. He makes you sit down 36 times. The fear, I may even say the terror, of not giving you a worthy reception puts him into a feverish agitation. He never stops talking and asks you a thousand questions without waiting for an answer. In short, nothing is too much trouble for him to show his friendliness, and it never occurs to him that so much painful effort makes him tiresome as well as tired.

But who would dare reproach him for what he is, since it's the most natural thing in the world for him not to be natural and the confidence and veneration which surround him are lawfully due him? At his dinner table, shared by some of his priests, he is the life and soul of the company. He interrupts everyone and spreads gaiety all around him. In the pulpit his voice is full, his gestures expressive and his phrasing most profound. In society, with all his apparent exuberance, he knows how to keep his own counsel and read other men while keeping himself impenetrable. Thus he is beloved and venerated, and people have confidence in him.

His flock are his children. Poor, for the most part, they can always find money when he seeks it for his convents, his colleges or his churches. He could easily have made himself the head of a political party. All Irish Newfoundland would obey the slightest sign from him. He has not been tempted. He has recognized that all his influence should serve only the cause of religion and that to use it to further the ambitions of a party would be to prostitute it.

In Newfoundland the role of Catholic Bishop is a noble role. He is the supreme director of convents and colleges where the younger generation of the island go to seek an education that, until then, was altogether foreign to them; and above all he is the patron of a great confraternity of men that, to a Frenchman, are a rather odd association. I would almost say grotesque were it not for the moral grandeur of their aim. By this I mean the temperance societies, which have grown up so extensively in all North America and its dependencies. They are a veritable league against drunkenness, or rather against alcohol.

Would you believe it? The triumph over this close enemy is so rapid that in the State of Maine, "total abstinence" is a law, part of the political constitution. In other words the selling of spirits or any other drink, beer or wine, which contains it, is legally forbidden in any part of the state. Rum shops or grogshops, which we call "un zinc," exist only as memories. In the country you may come across young people who have never heard of liquor or of a drunken man. Since drunkenness has been done away with, the number of crimes has been greatly reduced and prosperity has increased. This is the ideal, dreamed of and followed by all the countries of this part of America.

Newfoundland people, almost entirely sea-faring folk, look with fear on this passion for drink that clouds the mind and weakens the body, as if it were a monster emerging from the sea to devour them. Therefore they have hotly joined in this battle, aided by all the strength of the Catholic and Protestant clergy. The temperance societies are already in considerable strength through the number of their members and their zeal in spreading their beliefs.

One should see them on the great feast days going in procession to church. It is then the grotesque side appears. First of all, there is the band or orchestra of the society. No concert of cats, at their hour of nocturnal inspiration, could produce such sublime discords. A row of fine fellows, blasting through their trumpets at full lung power, shower the air with false notes; behind them marches the leader of the confraternity. Outside their overcoats they wear a scarf with the colours of their society. The scarf is large and long, nobly spread across the breast with its ends flapping at their thighs. Around their tall hats, a white veil is artistically tied and falls in a tail as long as that of an Arab horse, and that the wind lightly blows hither and thither.

In order to support the weight of so much piled up grandeur, the pompous leader, who wears his uniform with all the grace of a chimpanzee who had never worn one in his life before, leans on a staff decorated with bunches of ribbon of a most countrified style. Next follow the main body of the brotherhood and after them another band, more staves, and more temperance addicts, and after them another procession and maybe even a fourth. Oh God of Music!

But it is not for the vain pleasure of parading that the temperance societies were founded. They gather together at meetings, usually presided over by the clergy or members of parliament. They make speeches and they pass resolutions. The time is not far away when total abstinence will become the law in Newfoundland.

And don't think that all that is words only! Often, at a dinner, you will see young people who drink nothing but water. Not for all the world would they moisten their lips with a drop of wine or beer. Is this admirable or ridiculous? All I can say is that drink is the death of the Irish and Scotch fisherman and that it is an enemy that can't be fought with half measures. I may add that no matter what the ascendancy of the clergy over the temperance societies, they belong to no party, either religious or political. They are essentially national and independent. Besides, if the clergy are powerful in Newfoundland, it is not by intrigue, but because of the strong religious feeling of the people.

In no part of the world are the clergy so tolerant. They could scarcely be otherwise if a good understanding is to be maintained in a population half Catholic and half Protestant, and the ministers of any sect enjoy as much liberty themselves as they allow to their own flock. Father so-and-so will accept a cigar with as little ceremony as Captain such-and-such. They visit young ladies and, on occasion, drive out with them. They joke and gossip. It took my breath away, the first time I heard a girl say "Isn't Father so-and-so a darling? Isn't he charming? I'm crazy about him." They know that between them is an insuperable barrier. They know it will never be broken down. What harm then? And why forbid this harmless flirtation?

There are only two places where I have not met Catholic priests—at a skating rink and at a dance. But the theatres are not closed to them. There were priests, and even the Bishop himself, at a staging of "Patience" put on by the young folk of St. John's. Possibly they wouldn't have attended if the piece had been staged by strolling players; but why should the name of the actors change a principle? More especially as "Patience" is an operetta which has had an immense success in London and New York and has nothing in common with a mystery play or a tragedy. Possibly the criticism of the Protestant clergy pushes the Catholic priests to this easygoing attitude, which, I hasten to say, I am far from blaming.

Perhaps, indeed, it is simply that here we are in the golden age. I believe it may be that. When the flock have the faith of a coal-heaver, the shepherds can, without inconvenience, mingle in their ordinary lives. In Newfoundland the men are unlearned.

They never consider using their intelligence in the realms of thought. They use it only to keep their commercial accounts in double-entry. The women, who read a lot, are more cultivated. I have known many who are more familiar with our French literature than many young French girls brought up in a convent. But the Englishwoman is more poetically inclined than any other woman on earth, and religion is the most sublime poetry of all.

You should see the enthusiasm that brings them to the church when a mission is on. How long are these pious exercises, the sermon of Father A or Father Z. This is the subject of all conversation. They have learned their discourses by heart and they repeat them to one another. They admire them together as much for their literary quality as for being the word of God. If the missioner has condemned the waltz, then at the next ball you will see all the young Catholic girls glued to their chairs while their Protestant friends whirl around with all the more energy. Many of them remain bound by their promise for the whole season. It's true that flirting isn't a sin—and there are compensations. And so the good mission-fathers, who doubtless come to St. John's for their own edification, having nothing else to forbid to souls so innocent, are compelled to take from them the harmless pleasure of waltzing.

As for the young Protestant girls, I suppose there are no amusements their pastors can deprive them of since they, their pastors, deprive themselves of nothing. Saving a little more respect paid him and the cloth of his coat, the clergyman has nothing to distinguish him from other men. He goes into society, he dances, he laughs and jokes. His wife entertains and his daughters are passionately addicted to lawn tennis. I have no more to say of him in this chapter.

There is only one Anglican Bishop for the whole Island of Newfoundland and the Bermudas. Every four year he passes several months in that part of his diocese. In comparison there are three Catholic Dioceses. Despite the disproportion of territory, a Protestant Bishop is a much less important personage than his opposite number, which comes, I think, from the great divisions in the Protestant Church.

The evening of the Carnival was celebrated at the skating rink by a masquerade. The fear of ridicule that would ensue from tumbling a young lady on the ice had stolen from me the courage needed to learn to skate.

3

THEATRICAL ENTERTAINMENTS

J ANUARY 10th. Yesterday a troop of Christy Minstrels gave an entertainment in the concert hall of the Athenaeum. The subject is well worth a description. The Christy Minstrels—the most American of all things—specialize in the singing of Negro music and the interpretation of it in its native way. To get this effect they start off by blackening their faces. The orchestra, composed of brasses and drums, is formed up in tiers and the singers are lined up on each side.

Suddenly the music commences, one of the singers plays a tambourine or a guitar and at the same time indulges in loud cries which he accompanies with the most simian grimaces and ridiculous gestures. These become wilder and wilder, in fact almost frenzied. He jumps over his chair as if launched by a spring. He skims all over the stage in a diabolical sarabande, all the while singing, playing and making faces, he jumps, twirls, and pirouettes, throwing his legs and arms in all unexpected directions. Then he drops back in his chair, suddenly calm, breathing in a low voice a languorous air with his whole body moving in cadence to this gentle rhythm.

Just when he is finished and one expects silence, another singer from the opposite side, holding his belly in both hands, emits a formidable roar of laughter, squirming on his chair in spasms of clamorous hilarity. At first bewildered, his friends look at him stupidly, then swiftly—as if struck with a sudden contagion—all of them roll on their seats and express their gaiety in a storm of savage yells. Then all are silent as if by enchantment, and from each side are hurled jeers, puns and all sorts of nonsense.

This is pretty well what a minstrel show is like. Everything you can think of that is funny and absurd; funny at least for the first time. These crude exhibitions delight the Americans who, despite the refinement of their civilization, still have in them a trace of the Yankee—the Cossack of the American race.

In this same hall, or other similar ones, are held frequent concerts, sales-of-work, lectures and dances for charitable purposes by the numerous benefit societies, both Catholic and Protestant. Miss Fisher is the heart and soul of these concerts in which the young men and girls of the town also take part. They even sometimes stage comedies.

It was in this hall that Stuart Cumberland,[12] before appearing in Paris, first astonished us with his mysterious science. The American character was well displayed upon this occasion. Cumberland arrived from Canada where he had charmed the Marquis of Lorne and Princess Louise. He was adroit enough to get himself presented to the public of St. John's by the Prime Minister, Sir W.W. (K.C.M.G.).[13] That was enough for the Opposition Party to declare war on Cumberland, accusing him of all kinds of trickery and seeking to discredit him in the public eye. During all the length of his stay, the thought-reader was the object of the most live-ly controversy between the two political parties, each of which was represented in St. John's by a daily newspaper.

This reached such a pitch that he judged it necessary to defend himself publicly at the beginning of one of his sessions and showed himself an orator of no mean ability. Full of verve and energy and with a caustic tongue, he was so well able to flay his anonymous calum-niator that the latter was forced to abandon his *nom-de-plume* and come out in the open to reply to him. In short, as the show threatened to end in a riot, Cumberland demanded that the members of a committee of scrutiny be elected from the audience. The hall, whose

STUART CUMBERLAND. "During all the length of his stay, the thought-reader was the object of the most lively controversy between the two political parties, each of which was represented in St. John's by a daily newspaper."

sympathy he had gained, sent him only his opponents, accompanying each of them with an ironical cheer as they left their seats. It was thus under the eyes of men prejudiced against him that Cumberland repeated on that evening, with his customary success, these astonishing demonstrations that the whole world has seen him present since then.

Shrove Tuesday—The evening of the Carnival was celebrated at the skating rink by a masquerade. The fear of the ridicule that would ensue from tumbling a young lady on the ice had stolen from me the courage needed to learn to skate. It was therefore as a simple spectator that I watched, gliding on the ice, a host of Spaniards, Neapolitans, pierrots, dominoes of all shades and all the other great personages who form the escort of Prince Carnival.

I found there the elegant Miss Maud, who had her gown made in Paris, and her friend the pretty Miss Lilia. The latter was just back from London, where she had been studying. She had come home by the latest boat under the sole guard of her virtue and her 18 years. Maud introduced me to her friend and then skated lightly away to the end of the rink leaving me face-to-face with Lilia. She spoke little French but spoke that little with the simple grace she showed in all her actions. At first I thought myself in a difficult situation, thrown so abruptly into the arms of a new friend, but it was not the case. In truth, I had sworn not to let anything astonish me, but additionally the air of candour, which sat so deliciously on her lovely features, the intelligent glance of her clear eyes whose charm was augmented by her brown hair, established a sympathetic feeling between us almost at once.

Our conversation was most animated when the dismal music that passes here for a brass band attacked, or rather massacred, "God Save the Queen." It was the signal for the end, for no gathering, public or private, terminates here without the playing of the national anthem. As it is played, it is the custom to stand uncovered.

They opened the narrow door of the rink and a drift of snow blew into the hall as if to warn us to take our precautions against the storm before quitting our shelter. Outside the wind raged and swept from the ground, in thick whirlwinds, this terrible dust of icy snow which blinds and stifles at the same time.

Such was the violence of the gale that to get home safely we had all three to link arms and tramp along with closed eyes, holding tightly to one another. When we had arrived at Maud's house, we went in to await a lull in the storm. We looked just like three snowmen.

We go to the parlour. We warm ourselves and drink a cup of tea. There is no question of the parents, they are out or gone to bed, but in any case they wouldn't play us the unkind trick of interrupting us. Only Maud's brothers and sisters join us and then Lilia says "Let's dance." Everyone jumps to push a table or a chair out of the way to make a clear field and the dance commences. I thought that this evening I had learned the American Waltz, but since I no longer have Lilia for a partner, I find it impossible to remember the steps she taught me.

Towards midnight the weather was almost fine and I was honoured by escorting Miss Lilia home. During this walk we got to know each other and we found we had an infinity of mutual tastes. Arriving at her door we shook hands with the frank and natural gesture of two old friends whose confidence equals their affection. How far I am from France—and what a pity it is that France is not nearer America. Perhaps they *will* come closer together. Steam has already shortened the distance from Paris to New York. But the beautiful American girls of Paris are well on the way to destroying distance altogether. They are bringing to French women who don't wish to travel, what they would find abroad if fashion drove them there—a broadening of their minds.

Travel enlarges the personality, that's incontestable. I have ideas today about the codfish and seals such as no friend of mine in France can have…no matter how learned he may be.

At this time the preparations for the sealing voyage are the one thing on everybody's mind. Crowds gather around the latest steamer to arrive. The weather is watched anxiously.

4

A VOYAGE TO THE ICE

MARCH 3rd—The port and the town begin to show some activity. Instead of the wretches who hang about in winter and who congregate in St. John's to live on public charity, one sees a new breed of men; sturdy, energetic, with decision in their alert glance, red-whiskered and tall in their boots, who come to sign on for the fishery, or rather for the seal hunt.

The sealing steamers, those sea wolves, arrive from Scotland. They have had a long and dangerous passage. Day and night they have glided through the fog, their horns blaring continuously. Some of them may have met an ice-floe a dozen leagues long which lay across their route and have had to change course to avoid it. One of them, caught in a thick fog, found herself a prisoner in the ice, closely hemmed in and carried south, far from her goal.

ICEBERGS OFF THE HARBOUR OF ST. JOHN'S. "They have had to tack about for agonizing hours in the middle of hundreds of icebergs...that they shaved past with a horrible fear that they might tumble over on the steamer and crush it to bits."

Others, more fortunate, have been able to make their intended landfall. They have had to tack about for agonizing hours in the middle of hundreds of icebergs, some of them large and so flat that they can hardly be seen approaching, others lofty as mountains that they scarcely had time to avoid and that they shaved past with a horrible fear that they might tumble over on the steamer and crush it to bits.

Every year there are about a dozen of these brave craft which come from Scotland to outfit at St. John's for the seal fishery. They have their gear and their supplies in store and they sign on their crews in St. John's. The Scots have tried to man these vessels with their own countrymen, but have failed in this and have had to agree that the Newfoundlander is the only man who can take to the ice after the seals. It's almost as if it is in their blood, like their own Newfoundland dogs, who throw themselves in the water and swim there like ducks. It's a good thing they are like that, since the sealing industry, after the cod fishery, is the colony's greatest source of revenue.

For many years the sealing voyage was made only in sailing vessels. From St. John's alone, over a hundred such craft sailed every year to try their luck. The first steamer was introduced in 1863 and its success justified the innovation. Today, 20 years later, there are over 30 steamers which outfit here, while the sailing craft number no more than five or six. These steamers are built as strong as fortresses, especially in the bow, where there is a thick wall of iron-wood armoured with steel. The crew usually runs to between 200 and 300 men. As the steamer fishery usually does better, they can take their choice of applicants. They naturally take the young and strong; the others sign on the sailing vessels.

At this time the preparations for the sealing voyage are the one thing on everybody's mind. Crowds gather around the latest steamer to arrive. The weather is watched anxiously. From every outport, the newspapers get telegrams describing the appearance, favourable or otherwise, of the ice-fields around the island. They recall the results of the preceding year and they run to visit the steamers as if they were old friends found again after a long absence. In brief, there is a commercial turmoil in the town and as varied an interest as if an army corps were being mobilized for a military campaign.

Since the first of March, several sailing ships have set out, but by law the steamers cannot leave port until the tenth. Thus they arrive on the grounds about March 20th. This is the right time to take the young seals, then about three weeks old, loaded with fat and unable to escape as they have not yet learned to swim.

March 10th—On board the sealer *French Shore*.[14] The weather is perfect. It's a bright, frosty, sunny day. Our engines have steam up; they hoist the blue and white pilot's flag and I have just left my bag in the cabin that Captain Dickson has offered to share with me. There is no spare space in a sealing ship, only a cabin for the Captain, a forecastle for the men[15] and all the rest for the seals. We have 260 men on board. They came aboard yesterday, each with his mattress and coverings which they have lined up in the forecastle like herrings in a barrel. They don't need any wash-basin because they are forbidden to wash during the whole duration of the voyage.[16]

The screw begins to turn, breaking the sheet-ice around it. We are at the bottom of the harbour and to get out we must follow the channel cut in the ice and kept open by the incessant coming and going of a little green steam tug. I lunched with the Captain. He has always had good luck and hoped to show me a good voyage this time. It seemed the wind was in a good quarter. We turned the Cape on the north. They hoisted the mizzen sail and all the topsails to help the engines. This morning the coast was laced with fog and on leaving port we heard the siren on Cape Spear groaning dismally its continual warning. Later, a westerly wind arose and cleared away the fog and the ice pans.

We sailed on in complete freedom and the crew took advantage of this time to prepare for the hunt, getting ready their sealskin boots which came up to their knees and which have a thick leather sole armed with sparrow-bills. The rest of their equipment is a steel-shod gaff and a rifle.

March 17th—Imagine my surprise when I went on the bridge this morning and found we were painfully threading our way through a multitude of ice-cakes floating at water-level. During the night, there had been a swift change of wind which brought back against the coast the ice that had drifted off. The

Captain was desperately upset. He had counted on seeing a seal on every pan and not one was to be seen. The more the ice packed up, the more difficult became our progress and we pass all day in useless observations.

March 18th—The scene has changed again and resembles a fairytale at the Chatelet. Last night there was an intense frost that changed the sea into a field of ice. The fires were banked, we were definitely prisoners, but like prisoners who were robbers locked up in a palace full of treasures, for as far as the eye could reach we could see nothing but a teeming multitude of young seals. What a surprise: They are the most gentle creatures imaginable. They are scarcely three feet long and warmly wrapped in a thick coat of white fur, as white as new fallen snow, and they look at you with big, black, intelligent, gentle eyes.

CUTTING A CHANNEL IN THE ICE AT ST. JOHN'S TO FACILITATE THE DEPARTURE OF THE SEAL FLEET, MARCH, 1880. "The screw began to turn, breaking the sheet-ice around it. We are at the bottom of the harbour and to get out we must follow the channel cut in the ice and kept open by the incessant coming and going of a little green steam-tug."

All the men are on the ice where they run and jump with the ease of dancers on a waxed floor.

It's a shocking slaughter. No battlefield offers so moving a spectacle. With a telescope I follow the movements of the struggle and even our ship, her cordage and hull outlined in ice in every detail, is surrounded by carcasses. The hunter, armed with a gaff, jumps out on the ice and hits the young defenceless seal on the muzzle and it dies with the most plaintive and hopeless cries, real cries like a little child. It's enough to break one's heart and the few beginners we have are hesitant to strike a blow.

A horrible detail: as soon as the poor creature has been knocked out, with a knowing slash of a knife the executioner makes a slit from the throat to the tail and with a twist of the wrist the poor beast is deprived of its skin and its thick coat of fat. Often, excited like the tiger by the blood of its victim, the murderer rips out the heart, all warm and quivering, and tears it with his voracious teeth—Horror! The carcass, a tattered remnant of bloody flesh, is abandoned and the ice all around is splashed with flowing blood.

Imagine for yourself nearly 300 men all busy at this throat-slitting. On the sea, all frozen to the limit of visibility, are thousands of young seals, immobile and silent, and then in a moment one sees and hears the despair of these poor beasts, the lamentations that arise on all sides, the hideous and bloody skeleton which lies on the ice, filthy and steaming. The men, mad with slaughter, devour the living hearts of the victims or fill up their game bags with them. What barbarity!

But what of the poignant sorrow of the unhappy mother, the cries of fear? This violent manifestation of despair when, returning to the ice-hole near which she had left her infant to seek food, she finds nothing left but a lifeless wreck. Of all the tragic and revolting scenes of this drama, unique in the world, this is the worst. It might not be so bad if the seal was like other animals, but it isn't. It has an almost human cry and among animals, is one of the species with the most highly developed intelligence.

The mother's intelligence is marvellous. When she has dropped her only offspring on an ice field, she keeps a hole in the ice, near the pup, open to the sea, which enables her to seek food for herself and her young one. What does she do to prevent the ice blocking her passage? No one knows, but this is certain: observation has shown that she never makes a mistake in her blow-hole. Every time, she returns to the one near her pup and never confuses it with another. If the ice-field did not move it would not be surprising, in spite of so many other holes nearby, but, on the contrary, these masses are always on the march, influenced both by the wind and the ocean currents. The young seal stays six weeks on the ice, and at the end of this time its fur—which has

SEAL HUNTING OFF THE COAST OF NEWFOUNDLAND. "The men, mad with slaughter, devour the living hearts of the victims or fill up their game bags with them. What barbarity!"

given it the name of "white coat"—now becomes striped with dark splotches and it begins to take to the water.

The Captain has just given me the day's figures; they are splendid. Ten thousand, four hundred and some odd pelts. The men have cleared up the decks and formed in line and gone to dip their hard bread in a mug of tea as black as coffee. It's the only food on board except some salt pork three times a week; but all drinks except tea are rigourously forbidden. One must therefore excuse them for their appetite for seals' hearts, more particularly since their traditional eating of them is a preventive of scurvy.

Finally I explained to myself the indefatigable ardour of these brave fellows in killing from dawn to dusk! Instead of being on a salary, the crew get a share of the gross product of the voyage and the Captain gets a few cents per skin.

March 19th—We are still held prisoner, but the situation is not so good. All the seals for a mile around were killed yesterday and the men have to go a long distance to seek more. There is a lot of time lost in going and coming back with pelts, each of which weighs about 40 pounds. A man strings about five or six on a tow-rope and hauls them to the ship. When one has to cover a mile or two, with such a load to haul on slippery and lumpy ice, it's a task both tough and tiring. So today, we take aboard only about 3000 pelts.

March 20th—We had a violent storm last night. It was frightening. The ship, unable to yield to the wind, had to take the strain all standing. Everything groaned in the most sinister fashion and the wild gusts whistled through the icebound rigging, but we escape with only a little damage to our spars.

Alas. The storm has spared us only because it has found a victim elsewhere.

Daylight was about failing when 12 sealers from the steamer *Greenland*[17] came aboard to seek shelter from our Captain. The poor men were exhausted and could only satisfy our curiosity after they had been warmed and fed. They had walked part of the night—about the time that day steals from night in these regions—and all day without knowing where they were going or whether they were headed in the right direction or the wrong.

The tempest which had sprung up yesterday had fallen on them when they were killing seals about two miles from the *Greenland*. At first they were not uneasy, then the wind started rising and carried with it from the horizon a thick fog which suddenly swallowed them up. They started off, therefore, in what they thought was the direction of their ship. The storm increased and the sun threatened to lose itself in the ocean. Suddenly it emerged from the mist. The atmosphere recovered its limpid clearness and every pinnacle of ice reflected the last rays of its setting orb. But the steamer was no longer there and the unfortunates realized that they had gone astray in the fog. In fact, instead of keeping west, they had swerved and kept it on their left.

They looked everywhere but could see nothing. The stream of fog that enveloped them cut through in the middle a circle of which they were the centre and, in spite of their swift march, the night was even quicker and roughly swept away the last streaks of light. The wind rose higher, whirling the ice-dust that it lifted up in blinding clouds. Then it rose in a bank right up to the sky and drove before it with loud roarings great black heavy masses which burst in their flight and splashed down a fine rain edged with hard particles of hail. Totally lost, the survivors sought shelter at the base of an iceberg and crouched there, stung by the frost and menaced by the risk of falling ice.

Then the sun, scarcely set, soon rose again, slashing the horizon with a thin line of pale gold. One might have said that the wind recognized in it a stronger and superior being, because at the sight of it he lowered his voice and held back the torrent of his rage. The snow stopped falling and only rose in a flurry at rare intervals. The clouds, relieved of their weight, rose high in the sky that they veiled without hiding; part of the horizon, which is all of ice, reaches out to the open water.

But where is the *Greenland*? They might well search for it! The castaways cannot find any sign of her, not even a wisp of smoke to indicate her hidden behind an iceberg. They consulted the compass and, the position of the ship being decided, they set out for her. In a moment they found the heap of seal pelts that they had piled up when the storm forced them into flight. There was no more doubt, they were on the right road, but they should be able to see the steamer, unless the tempest has freed her from the ice and forced her out into the open sea.

CAUGHT IN THE ICE FIELDS OF THE NORTH ATLANTIC. "There was nothing left of the ship but a few planks, some splintered spars and a few rope ends…the steamer had been crushed and smashed to bits under the fall of a mountain of ice."

Everybody's glance swept the horizon, but nothing was to be seen. The ice field was broken up in many places. In a space of a thousand yards one had to jump from one pan of ice to another. There was one poor chap, the youngest, who was so tired out that his foot slipped and they had to fish him out. This seemed a bad omen to everyone. Up to then, they had not dared to face their fear, but now a voice cried out. "There must have been some disaster. We can't be more than a quarter of a mile away and we should be able to see her!" Every man felt terror clutch at his heart. This was the expression of their inner thoughts but so far no one had had the courage to say so. Suddenly they stopped short simultaneously, unable to utter a word or to make a step.

The mystery is at last unveiled. A hundred yards ahead of them is where the *Greenland* had been! After the moment of shock which had held them, a ray of hope arose and they hurried to the fateful spot. There was nothing left of the ship but a few planks, some splintered spars and a few rope ends. The way they were buried in the ice eloquently conveyed that the steamer had been crushed and smashed to bits under the fall of a mountain of ice. And the same voice that had already spoken, declaimed "If they're down there, only God can help them. As for us, let's try to save ourselves."

Then it was that their situation in all its horror stared them in the face like an apparition rising from the grave in which their ship was entombed. Where could they go? What could they do? And what could they hope for? "We have only one chance of safety," said an old-timer, "and that's to reach land over the ice." But the wind was blowing offshore. There must be open water near the coast. "Maybe we'll be seen by some boat, what other chance have we?"

They set out towards the west. A few seals gave their hearts and livers to form a menu for lunch and they tried to wash it down with a handful of snow. After some hours spent in jumping from one ice pan to another among a host of seals, they at last reached a huge ice field which stretched all in one piece as far as the eye could reach. At this sight everyone regained hope. However, they still had to walk for twelve hours before they glimpsed the faint smoke of the *French Shore* which had re-fired her furnaces in the hope of a break up. Shortly after the lucky discovery of this smoke there came into view some of our sealers who were farthest from the ship.

At this point, sure now of being rescued, the feverish energy that had driven them forward in a flight from death suddenly left them. They fell down, worn out with fatigue and joy, feeling that they could not move another step. But the old-timer, still on his feet, shouted, "Keep going," and a supreme effort brought them to the steamer and to the mugs of hot tea they needed so badly.

March 21st—We are clear at last. As soon as we could worm a passage we steamed towards the place where the *Greenland* had been. We found under the ice the wreckage told of by the castaways, but because of the drift of the ice it happens that these relics were far from marking where the *Greenland* had gone down. The only question now is whether the crew saved themselves or not. So our siren never ceased hurling its powerful signal to the wind, stopping only to let the voice of the cannon be heard. Rockets and Bengal flares were made ready for the night.

All that doesn't prevent our men from carrying out a most active hunt. As the *Greenland* survivors had led us to expect, we found ourselves in the midst of a great host of seals. But the scene had for me a totally new interest. It was no longer a matter of running over the solid surface of the sea. Now there were thousands of ice pans floating freely around, gently rocked by the waves. And, lightly, with almost contemptuous skill, in spite of looking as clumsy as leather-clad bears, our sealers leap from one floe to another, kill their seal, and perform the operation as nonchalantly as a cook cutting up a beefsteak on a kitchen table.

Yesterday it was a drama; today it is a tragicomedy. The actors are a seal of the hood species and three sealers. First, a few words on the hoods.[18] They are the biggest and least plentiful of the seal species, although less valued than the harp seals. The male carries on his head a thick mass of elastic tissue which he can inflate over his eyes and nose like a monk's hood, from which he derives his name of "hood" or *capuchon*. So helmeted, he is proof against the blows of the gaff, and the only means to finish him off is to lodge a bullet in his ribs a little behind the head. This animal defends himself when attacked and will himself savagely attack to save the life of his female and little one.

Now when a man finds himself on a pan with a young hood, he greets him with a blow on the nose with his gaff. At the victim's cry, the father leaps from the water, furious, and shoots forward against his enemy with his hood lowered. Two more sealers fly to help their comrade. Gaff blows hail down on the seal's head, but inspired with hate, the valiant beast faces each of them and rushes, jaws open and reaching for an arm, catches on the swing one of the gaffs and shatters it with his teeth. Disarmed, the combatant retreats, so hard pushed that, without time to turn, he falls into the sea. It's all up with the man if the seal takes to the water, so the two other men bar his passage, attracting the rage of the monster to themselves while their comrade finds his feet again. Then they execute a retreat behind a barrage of gaff-blows. A sealer armed with a rifle arrives in time to decide this battle, but it is only by good luck that tragedy did not plunge his dagger in a purer blood than a seal's.

March 22nd—Have the crew of the *Greenland* perished entirely or have they been picked up by another ship? We have lost all hope of coming up with them. Nonetheless we continue to sound our alarm whistle every half hour. Today's hunt has brought to 30,000 the number of sealskins stowed on board. It's magnificent. Excepting our cabin and the men's forecastle, we are as full as an egg from keel to deck. We need only take advantage of the fine weather and hurry back to port, but our good Captain Dickson would not get underway without making one more sweep to look for the *Greenland*'s crew. All our sealers are on board and we start out on the search.

March 23rd—About five o'clock this morning, the *French Shore* is at the edge of the ice. Beyond it is open water all the way to France. We are returning on our track, or rather on our wake. There is nothing more to be done for the *Greenland*'s crew. Back in the ice we were surrounded by such a herd of seals that we couldn't help making another attack on them. At the day's end there were 7000 more pelts on board—37,000 skins, each with about three inches of fat. Where to put them? There wasn't much hesitation. With one voice the crew offered the forecastle. The Captain expands in triumph.

March 27th—We arrived at St. John's. We questioned the pilot but he knew nothing of the *Greenland* disaster. We had a very good return trip, in spite of the cold. The men have passed four nights on deck rolled in their blankets, but that didn't keep them from being in the best of spirits and the best of health. Next morning we began to unload the steamer. They scraped the fat from the skins which will be salted for export to England where they are used to make shoes, harness, luggage etc. As for the fat, it's cut up into small pieces by a steam machine, melted down, and then exposed to the sun in great vats under glass. The end product is a pale oil, odourless and refined, which is exported for making fine soaps, and also used in lighthouses, machines and other things. A tun of this oil is worth about $140.00, and the skin of a young harp about a dollar.

April 14th— On the report of Captain Dickson, the Government has sent a steamer to seek for the castaways of the *Greenland*. It got back this morning but had discovered nothing. Three hundred men were lost. No one could remember a comparable disaster.

Of all the sealers that had returned to port, the *French Shore* had the quickest trip and the biggest catch. There were two ships that had been caught in the ice quite near here and had brought back only two or three hundred seals each. They were getting ready to go out again. The *French Shore* sails again tomorrow to tempt fortune a second time. This time they will be hunting adult seals who can swim and won't wait patiently to be knocked on the head and skinned and therefore the gaff is replaced by the rifle.

April 15th—God be praised, 70 men of the *Greenland*'s crew have turned up this morning on a sailing vessel. Forty-three others were rescued by another sailing craft and are on their way to St. John's. According to their account the 27 men, including the Captain, who remained on board, perished with the steamer. As for the survivors, they were saved on the following day. While we were looking for them, they were on the sailing vessels that a contrary wind had driven seawards. St. John's went wild with joy.

Coming out of Mass, I accompanied Miss
Gertrude to the cottage of one of her married
sisters. There are four sisters, three of them
married, each one more charming than the other.

5

THE YOUNG NEWFOUNDLAND WOMAN

MAY 30th—Let us come back to our young Americans, or rather our young Newfoundlanders. My old sense of surprise has melted with this winter's snow. I find this liberty and camaraderie with young ladies to be altogether natural. It seems, though, that if I have changed my habits, I have not changed my nature. How many times have I heard it said "How French you are."

MISS LUCRETIA STABB. *"I often go in the evenings to chat with one or another of my numerous lady friends, and rarely do we stop talking or playing music before eleven o'clock."*

It is claimed that we French people have a monopoly on gallantry and therefore, over here, the most insignificant Parisian is sure of easy success in society. To some extent, it's the fault of the young men of Newfoundland. Why is their education so inferior to that of their sisters? Manual work is unknown to young ladies. You'll never find them with a needle or crochet-hook in their hand. Walks, lawn tennis, lectures and tea-parties are their daily occupations, while their brothers, hats on the backs of their heads, work in an office or preside over the business of their firm. Thus, apart from the public officials, all the respectable men are in commercial life.

I often go in the evenings to chat with one or another of my numerous lady friends, and rarely do we stop talking or playing music before eleven o'clock. It is well known that the English are crazy about music, although they hear it less than any. Everyone can recognize an English air at the first bar. Every English person, male or female, thinks they can sing and that they have a voice whether they have or not. Mostly they have not, and limit themselves to ejaculating a few sounds like a succession of sighs. They know this very well, and it's enough that one is French to have it laid on one as a duty to have a melodious voice. They torment you, they beg you for a ballad, and it's no use your swearing that you can't sing, they just don't believe you.

How many times have I applauded at the end of a piece during the rendering of which I suffered martyrdom in not being able to plug my ears, when I had to make the most furious effort not to burst out laughing. Naturally there are exceptions. Very few indeed but still some, apart from Miss Fisher, and I tend to visit by preference the homes where conversation replaces music.

Yesterday, I passed the evening *tête-à-tête* with lovely Kitty, her sister Betsy having gone on a trip. We parted about midnight having dealt lightly with many subjects: love, literature, even philosophy, if you please. Perhaps it would be to the point to note some details of this memorable conversation. We will find in it most of the traits needed to form a convincing portrait of the young Newfoundland girl.

As I was strolling without power to decide on a definite route, I ran into Miss Kitty coming out of church. "Let's take a walk in the moonlight," she said to me.

"Willingly. We are only a step or two from Quidi Vidi. Let's go and see the moon in the lake. How is your sister? Will she be home soon?"

"No. She has postponed her return. She seems to be amusing herself there quite a bit. She has written me a long letter, and here is a note for you that she included in it. Look at the lovely sky. I've never seen so many stars before, or so brilliant a moon. We can walk all around the lake, if you wish."

"Good Lord! What's wrong with you? Three miles in slushy snow?"

"That's true. I didn't think of that. You see, I'm so happy."

"I can see that if you went to church to compose yourself, you've not been very successful."

"If you knew what's happened you wouldn't tease so. All right! I'll tell you everything. I'm engaged."

"Look, you've knocked a star out of the sky."

"Oh, you are tiresome! You'll bring me bad luck."

"All right, tell me since when and to whom."

"To Dick Stephens, who's been here the last eight days."

"Yes, and who's going away tomorrow on the mail boat."

"Well, what do you think of him?"

"He's very fortunate! And how long have you known him?"

"Oh, for a long time, only he left Newfoundland when he was very young and for 17 years we didn't see each other."

"Seventeen years! And you're only 20!"

VIEW FROM THE NORTH SIDE OF QUIDI VIDI LAKE. "We are only a step or two from Quidi Vidi. Let's go and see the moon in the lake."

"That's true, I was only three years old, but I remember at that age, I was mad about him."

"And you have had the patience to wait until now to tell him so."

"Now, now! Don't make fun of me. This is all very serious, we met again— and we fell in love, a thunder-stroke."

"There you are, delighted: you dreamed a romance and everything came true like a stage-play."

"Lord, but these Frenchmen are teasers! Quiet now. I won't let you talk any more about it, you are laughing at love!"

"That's your fault. There's nothing less poetic than to have one's feet wet!"

"Well let's go back, but if you have the misfortune to talk prose to me, I'll turn you out."

"I'll equalize it by asking Poetry to open the window."

In a moment we came to Kitty's house. The coals were glowing in the parlour grate and there were no lights. The chimney-piece was bordered with a band of fabric that threw moving shadows on the floor.

"I love to sit in a room lit only by a fire," said Kitty as she went in.

"I was opening my mouth to say the same thing."

"Then don't let's light the lamp. We'll talk better this way."

It was a warm evening and thawing outside. The fire served more to take up the damp than to combat the cold. We opened a window and sat on the window seat.

Nothing is so conducive to dreaming as a window open at night on a clear sky brilliant with stars. So, after a minute, leaning against each other, we had flown into space, landing in turn on the farthest suns and the most radiant planets. We argued over the impression created by the contemplation of these splendours.

"This elevates the soul" she said. "One feels capable of great deeds. How could one, in the face of such majesty, succumb to unworthy temptations? It is true that one feels the sweet thought of love arise in one, but of a love pure, ethereal and divine!"

I thought exactly the opposite. "If you feel elevated," I said, "I feel myself oppressed. At first I let myself be carried away by the poetry of admiration. I go ahead, lost in enthusiasm, until I suddenly find myself dizzy with horror of the void. Horror kills the sense of poetry. Mystery stifles admiration. There remains only infinity, the terrible unknown which devours everything, the universe as well as the human mind. Come back from so far away. How can one look on one's self without fear and pain? You," I added, "have in your hand a thread that will guide you back to this world, so I understand that you feel less strongly than I. You have a perfect right to such flights if you wish."

"Now, now! If you're going to look for bad luck even in the stars, let's close the window."

Then to get my own back, I put a light to a gas-jet and took up a book from the table. It was The *Lady of the Camellias* that she had asked me for some days before. That, naturally, directed the conversation to literature, and she quoted to me some verses of Musset and Hugo, more particularly Musset, the poet beloved by all lovers. Then she asked me if life in France is the way it is depicted in our abominable novels. When I told her that all she read was only a feeble drawing of the reality, her instinct as a woman in love revolted at the idea that love itself was the cause of so many crimes and betrayals.

"If you don't believe me," I said in leaving, "at least believe your own poet Tennyson: 'Never morning wore/ To evening, but some heart did break'."— and delighted to have found these verses to reply to her French quotations, I translated it into French. A minute later the Northern Lights held us both enchanted, standing in the middle of the street bathed in a stream of poetry.

It was the hour when forgotten souls return to earth; the hour of the witches' Sabbath; the hour of love; the sinister and charming hour of midnight. Not a wisp of cloud floated in the air; not a breath of wind stirred. The moon slept at the bottom of the lake, and from the top of the hill which hangs over the centre of a great circle, the town swept down to the silent harbour.

Like the keystone of a huge dome, a silvery light spread out to the middle of the heavens. It was splashed with pale green flames against the dark mass of the hills and made a fairy-like halo at the horizon. The north was lightly rose-coloured and sometimes a pale green streak shot out—perhaps, we said, a soul delivered from the clay and mounting to God. The stars, piercing these thin filaments, glittered like precious stones set in a giant burst of glory. A flash died out here, another shot out elsewhere. Turn by turn, long streaks of light blazed and suddenly vanished.

Suddenly the movement quickened. The great dome dissolved its majestic architecture. The thousands of light-rays, a moment ago crowded and ranged in circles, danced away in space, mounted, fell, soared, chased themselves from one corner of space to another like a fantastic ballet, in a shower of dancing forms. Perhaps also, by Odin's orders, the souls of old Frankish warriors celebrated a tournament in heaven, the forgotten anniversary of some heroic victory.

Sunday June 24th—Coming out of Mass, I accompanied Miss Gertrude to the cottage of one of her married sisters. There are four sisters, three of them married, each one more charming than the others. One of them is the pretty person in white who wore a bunch of red roses at the Government House Ball. Having drunk a glass of port and picked some early pansies, we went back to St. John's, admiring the fresh verdure that the country had assumed in casting off its mantle of snow.

"Can you guess," said Miss Gertrude, "what I dreamed last night? That the *Clorinda* had arrived and that I was shaking hands with the Captain." Just as she finished a signal was made by the semaphore and after a moment's scrutiny I saw that it announced a French war-ship.

"Mademoiselle," I said, "your dream is realized." Half an hour after, the *Clorinda* was anchored in the harbour and soon a fine whale-boat, all white, shot out from her, proudly flying the French colours among the English fishing fleet. Suddenly the eight oars disappeared simultaneously, like a bird folding its wings, and the boat came alongside the Queen's Wharf. Two officers, sent by the Captain of the Flagship of the French Newfoundland Naval Squadron stepped ashore and we took together the road to the Consulate.

From there we went to see the Governor.[19] He came, preceded by a villainous odour of ether. In spite of his black hair and side-whiskers, his forehead is marked with premature age. Who would think, seeing him today feeble and bent under the weight of his great frame, that this man of 51 had ridden in the great charge at Balaclava? He was named Governor of Newfoundland two years ago and only assumed his responsibilities recently, being prevented from taking up his post by illness. He belongs to one of the best families in England, and from his long service in the great courts of Europe he was, at the same time, a friend of Prince Bismarck and Admiral Fourichon.

The officers of the *Clorinda* were come to ask him if he wished them to fire a salute of 21 guns as a Royal salute. But in the absence of any English warship there were no guns available to reply to the *Clorinda* and the ceremony was postponed until later.

HENRY BERKELEY FITZHARDINGE MAXSE. "He came, preceded by a villainous odour of ether. In spite of his black hair and side-whiskers, his forehead is marked with premature age.

A cat would have plenty of space in a room with a rat, but that wouldn't stop her eating it. This mixing of your fishermen with ours would be the cause of continuous quarrels.

6

PARLIAMENT AND THE FRENCH FISHERIES DISPUTE

J UNE 29th—I lunched this morning in the Officers' Mess, which I do nearly every day. After leaving the table, two or three of the company came ashore with me, and as the notorious problem of the fisheries was the subject of our discussion, I suggested to a junior officer, a friend of mine, that we should make a call on the Colonial Secretary. This is how we spent the day.

Climbing to the top of the hill we found ourselves facing the Parliament House. We crossed the courtyard and climbed the dozen steps to the raised first floor of the building. This floor is almost entirely occupied by two assembly rooms decorated in relief. One is the chamber of the elected Assembly, the other of the Legislative Council, or Upper House.

At this point many of my readers will be astonished at these terms. We have no such governmental setup in France. With us, everything is centralized to excess. Réunion and Martinique are only distant provinces. But an independent colony governing itself! What a strange phenomenon! That's how it is, though, and here is the parliamentary history of Newfoundland from its beginning in a few words.

In 1832, representative government and a constitution were granted to Newfoundland. The Island was divided into nine districts, each of which, depending on its population, named one or two members. In all about 15 and no more. Every man could vote, who, on election day, had for a year been a tenant or householder on the island. At the same time a Legislative and Executive Council was created. It was composed of seven members, nominated by the Crown.

The system functioned badly. The constitution was suspended. The Council was abolished as a distinctive branch of the Legislature and its ex-members were authorized to sit and vote in the Assembly similarly to the elected members. This new arrangement was called "The Amalgamated Legislature."

But in 1847 the Imperial Government laid the foundations of the Colonial Building, as the Parliament House is called. A hundred thousand dollars were spent and in 1850 the Legislature took its seat there for the first time. Doubtless the pride of seeing themselves in such a sumptuous edifice went to the heads of the members of this noble assembly. Their houses of wood seemed marble palaces and the miserable fishing coves seemed superb and powerful seaports. In brief—on the direct demand of the people—Responsible Government was demanded and obtained.

In 1855 this new and last transformation took place. The English garrison with its artillery was withdrawn from St. John's. The Newfoundlanders believed, and remain more convinced than ever, that a new power had arisen in the world. This is the present system—the one that has functioned now since 1855. First, there are two chambers, the lower, the House of Assembly, elected by the people, and the upper, the Legislative Council, nominated by the Governor in Council.

The Governor, who is the sole direct representative of the sovereign, is sent by the Crown and his tour of duty is usually for six years. The House of Assembly is composed of 33 members elected every four years by the votes of the people. As in the past, to be an elector it is necessary to be, on election day, a tenant or householder for the preceding year. Fifteen members, named for life by the Governor in Council, form the Legislative Council. The Executive Council—seven members chosen by the majority party in the House—completes this governmental system. Up to 1883 there were only 15 electoral districts, but in this year two more were created in that part of the island known as the French Shore.

In order to run as a candidate, an aspirant must have an annual income of $480, or own property clear of encumbrance to the amount of $2400. It is mandatory, as well, that he should have lived on the island for two years before the election, be over 21, and be an English subject by birth or naturalization. The members of both branches of the legislature receive an honorarium. The titles of the great public officials who compose the Executive Council are: The Colonial Secretary—who is also the Secretary of the Executive Council—the

Attorney General, the Receiver General, the Surveyor General, the Financial Secretary, etc.

Now that we know all the titles of this imposing machine, let us try to see the effects and results that it produces, and first of all let us make contact with some of these gentlemen. In the Colonial Building itself is the office of the Colonial Secretary. Next to the Prime Minister—"The Honourable the Premier"—he is the most important personage in the Government. His post corresponds to that of a Minister of Foreign Affairs. For a long time this office has been filled by the Hon. Edward D'Alton-Shea, born in Ireland of a noble and ancient family—of which one branch became French—who came to

THE COLONIAL BUILDING. "A hundred thousand dollars was spent…doubtless the pride of seeing themselves in such a sumptuous edifice went to the heads of the members of this noble assembly."

Newfoundland about 30 years ago. Thanks to his brother, whose influence and prestige quickly spread through the country, he attained the eminence he enjoys today.

We will pay him a visit together, if you wish. He is an affable man of good presence and no one in Newfoundland knows better than he how to sustain the dignity of a rank which often brings him in contact with distinguished visitors. Beneath a cool and unemotional manner there lies an impartial judgment actuated by no party spirit. Honesty and sincerity shine through the prudent reserve of his speech. We found in this personage more healthy good-sense and genuineness than in any of his colleagues in authority and because of that, I propose to question him in your presence on the ancient and important problem of the French fisheries in Newfoundland.[20]

EDWARD D'ALTON SHEA. "Thanks to his brother, whose influence and prestige quickly spread through the country, he attained the eminence he enjoys today."

"May I present my friend Mr. –."

"Mr. Shea, Colonial Secretary."

"My friend, sir, is most anxious to talk with you on the subject of the French Shore and if you have some moments to spare…"

"Certainly, with pleasure, but you must understand that I can't say anything official. That subject is in the sphere of the Governor exclusively."

"Doubtless: and we ourselves are only visitors and tourists anxious to have a personal conversation with you for our own instruction. If you'll allow me to make my friend conversant with the history of the question, I will read you a little leaflet published in Quebec in 1876. In spite of its being eight years old, I will wager it is not in your governmental archives. It's too well-done and shows too clearly the justice of our claims; although it was written by an Englishman. Afterwards we can discuss the present state of affairs. Here it is. It's a reply to a publication issued in London and written by a lawyer from Nova Scotia named Whitman.[21] The following is quoted from the Quebec pamphlet:

The author (Mr. Whitman) established that the treaties of Utrecht (1713) and Versailles (1783) renewed by that of 1815 conferred on the French *no exclusive right of fishing* in Newfoundland waters; that accordingly the control that they presume to exercise in these seas is unjustifiable and that a French monopoly and jurisdiction in Newfoundland could not be longer tolerated and that their existence is *a limitation of the sovereignty of the English Crown.*

At the risk of seeming lukewarm patriots we will allow ourselves to oppose to this theory some objections drawn from history and in the very text of the treaties.

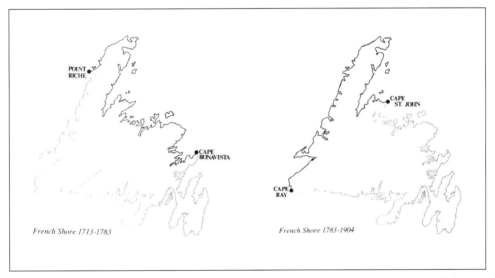

French Shore 1713-1783

French Shore 1783-1904

THE FRENCH SHORE 1713-1783 AND THE FRENCH SHORE 1783-1904. "You English are forbidden to fish on the part of the coast reserved to us. You have even less right to put up shore establishments as no settlement is permissible."

All the world knows that the Island of Newfoundland was first settled by the French. The evidences of this colonization are still visible everywhere in the names of places and also in some of the population since the island contains, to this day, 20,000 inhabitants of French speech and origin. A European coalition forced France to surrender Newfoundland and Acadia (now Nova Scotia) to England, reserving for her only a right of fishing in the bays and on the coasts of Newfoundland. At this time, all the islands at the mouth of the St. Lawrence remained peopled by colonists of French origin, and this situation lasted until the middle of the 18th century, since in 1755 the English believed themselves obliged to deport *en masse* the Acadian people to the number of nine or ten thousand souls in order to assure their own establishment.

There was not, in our opinion, during all this period any discussion between the two powers on the French fisheries or the monopoly. The monopoly sprang from the nature of things and in the logic of events. It was probably not even discussed until 1763. At this point only did the conflict commence. France had surrendered all its American possessions excepting two little islands, St. Pierre and Miquelon and its fishing rights, the poor crumbs of its colonial empire. Was this right exclusive: was it granted by England as a simple concession or as a monopoly? This point can only be clarified for us by considering all the facts. As proof of the negative, the reporter of the Colonial Institute cites Article V of the treaty of 1783 which confirms to the French their right of fishing such as it was laid down in the treaty of Utrecht. He adds that all subsequent treaties have simply and purely repeated the same clause. He runs through all these conventions without seeing any trace of an exclusive right for the French. From whence comes this conclusion that their monopoly in Newfoundland and the adjacent waters has never been anything but an unfounded claim. These citations are exact, but it might be useful to complete them by some minor additions. Let us explain first the historical facts.

The treaty of 1783 was not concluded by the two powers under the same conditions as that of 1763. France had by then taken a brilliant revenge on her rival and had shattered her colonial empire by forming a Republic out of her richest and most important colonies. In place of imposing a peace,

England had sought it as a favour and thought herself lucky to save some shreds of ancient possessions in America. There was general astonishment that France did not profit from her advantage to obtain some important restitutions in America or in the Indies.

At Paris and Versailles, M. De Vergennes was accused of weakness and to satisfy to some extent this surge of public opinion, French diplomacy insisted to the English Cabinet that Article V of the treaty expressly reserved to the French the exclusive right of fishing in the zone assigned to them. But the English minister strove to elude this recognition for fear of attracting to himself a too-violent attack in Parliament. Then a compromise term was adopted by the two powers to avoid the difficulty, while at the same time, giving France what she asked. At this stage, a declaration and a counter-declaration were signed by the respective plenipotentiaries and joined to the body of the treaty.

The *first of these declarations* contained the following stipulation that no international instrument has modified up to now.

"To the end that the fishermen of both nations be not involved in daily quarrels, His Britannic Majesty will take THE MOST POSITIVE measures so that his subjects will not disturb in any manner BY THEIR JOINT fishing the fishery of the French during the temporary exercise of the rights accorded them; and for this purpose will take away the shore establishments already constructed.

"Further on in the same declaration one may read:

"There will be no infringement of the usual method of fishing by either party: the subjects of His Britannic Majesty will not molest the French fishermen during their fishery, NOR INTERFERE WITH THEIR FLAKES DURING THEIR ABSENCE.

"These are, for all impartial judges, clauses both very clear and very explicit by which the King of England limited his sovereignty in Newfoundland as formally as did Louis XIV in 1713 when he undertook to destroy the fortifications and break down the port of Dunkirke.

"A text so precise, so categorical, applied to an enjoyment that was uncontested and almost time-honoured, leaves little room for discussion. One can see now what are the foundations of the French claims and if the English journals are justified in treating the descendants of Cartier and Champlain as intruders and pirates in the seas of Newfoundland.

"Let us see now what has been the interpretation of the treaty of 1783 between the two contracting parties for the last ninety-two years.

"We are come to the second paragraph of this little work. I still have seven or eight pages to read. Have you the patience to listen to the rest?"

"Certainly, go ahead, it's vividly interesting."

"Right. I'll continue."

"After the treaty of 1783, the monopoly of the French fishermen was exercised in a manner never contested in Newfoundland for a period of nine years and a half. This 10-year tenure of possession has a high significance in the debate and provides a strong argument in favour of the French system. Isn't it clear, indeed, that all disagreement between the negotiator on the spirit of the annexed declaration, produced immediate consequences and left indications either in the diplomatic correspondence or in the Archives of the two Navies in the Colonial records. The intention of the French in insisting on the clause was clear and they interpreted it immediately in the widest sense behind the protection of a navy that had just fought a victorious battle against the fleets of Britain. The English had raised no objection. No action, no restriction on their part, had disturbed the monopoly claimed by France and the methods by which they implemented it. The French had therefore in their favour, from the beginning, the two conditions needed for *Plenum Dominium* or full possession, namely:

(1) A clear title.

(2) Entry into possession and long enjoyment without any protest.

The year 1793 saw the opening of a state of war between the two nations, interrupted only by the short Peace of Amiens and concluded after twenty three years by the treaty of 1815. During this long struggle the French fishing rights in Newfoundland were necessarily in suspension; but we see that they were energetically reclaimed at every negotiation with England. The Treaty of Amiens in 1801, that of 1814 and that of 1815, invariably gave them back the rights they enjoyed in 1792: that is to say the benefit of the clauses stipulated in 1783. It is said that in 1815, wishing to get some material advantage out of Waterloo, England resolved to take one of her last colonial possessions from France and gave the Government of Louis XVIII the choice between the Islands of St. Pierre and with them the Newfoundland fisheries and the Isle de France now the Island of Mauritius. The Duke of Richlieu, in our opinion, by a happy inspiration opted for the American fisheries. Consequently the French monopoly was restored in all its primitive integrity and England showed a meritorious honesty in respecting it.

"But a totally new difficulty now met the French in the exercise of their rights. It was the opposition of the Colony itself. Newfoundland had developed greatly since the end of the 18th century. She could not see the re-establishment of a monopoly which arrested her expansion without a violent and very natural objection. It was hard for her fishermen to deprive themselves of the use of their bays, rich in fish, and not even be able to build upon their own coasts because of arrangements made by two far-off powers. Were they not the proprietors and the masters of the soil?"

Mr. Shea—dreamily. "Yes, yes."

"What were these Frenchmen, if not *strangers* and *intruders*?"—such was the logic of the legislature and the press of Newfoundland for 60 years. It is in general that of all Americans who have kindly permitted Europe to consecrate to their service their gold, their armies and their fleets; but who find it exorbitant that they should dare to limit their liberty of action at rare intervals.

From this moment onwards Newfoundland presents a singular phenomenon, namely a diverging of views between the Colony and the central authority on the validity and enforcement of treaties. England, conscious of her engagements, respects the rights of France and endeavours to assure her enjoyment of them. The Newfoundland colonists protest, inventing a theory that limits the treaty of Versailles and claims to modify official diplomacy. Deaf to the advice of the administration and of all maritime authorities, they insist on treating the French as trespassers, repealing in especial the annexed declaration and wishing to release England from its engagements.

This theory is stressed, for the first time in a very curious document, that the report of the Colonial Institute discreetly omits, and for good reason. We wish to speak of a proclamation of Sir Charles Hamilton, Governor and Commander in Chief of the Island of Newfoundland and its dependencies dated August 12, 1822.

Here is the proclamation:

By His Excellency Sir Charles Hamilton, Governor and Commander in Chief in and over the Island of Newfoundland and its dependencies.

A Proclamation

Whereas by the 13th Article of the Definite Treaty of Peace between His Majesty and the King of France, signed at Paris on the 30th May, 1814, it was stipulated that the French right of fishing upon the Great Bank of Newfoundland, upon the Coasts of the Island of that name, and of the adjacent islands in the Gulf of St. Lawrence should be replaced upon the footing on which they stood in 1792; which said 13th Article was again confirmed by the 11th Article of the definite Treaty between Great Britain and France signed at Paris 20th November 1815: And whereas the right of fishing preserved to the subjects of His Most Christian Majesty by the Treaty of Utrecht extends from Cape St. John on the East Coast of Newfoundland, and going round by the North and down the Western Coast, is bounded by Cape Raye:

And whereas representation has been made to me that depredations have been committed upon, and annoyances given by British Subjects to the French fishery within the said limits, I, the Governor aforesaid, do by this my Proclamation hereby make known that the subjects of His Most Christian Majesty are to have full and complete enjoyment of the fishery within the limits and boundaries aforesaid, in the manner they are entitled to enjoy the same under the said Treaty of Utrecht. And to this end all Officers, Magistrates and others under my Government, are hereby strictly enjoined that they do in their several stations, and as far as depends on each of them respectively, prevent any obstructions or interruptions, under any pretence, being given to the subjects of France in the enjoyment of the said Fishery, and that they, the said Officers and Magistrates do give them all reasonable countenance therein.

And Notice is hereby given to all His Majesty's subjects resorting to the part of the Coast of Newfoundland before described, that they are not to interrupt in any manner the aforesaid fishery of the subjects of His Most Christian Majesty within the limits above mentioned.

And in case any of His Majesty's subjects shall refuse to depart from that part of the Coast, within a reasonable time after receiving notice so to depart, the Officers under my orders are to cause any Stages, Flakes, Train Vats, or other works whatever erected by them for the purpose of carrying on the said fishery, to be removed, and also all Ships, Vessels and Boats belonging to them, within the limits aforesaid: And the said Officers are hereby required to use such means as may be found necessary for compelling His Majesty's subjects to depart from that part of the Coast of this Island, and to inform them, as they are hereby informed, that they will be prosecuted in the Courts of Law for such their refusal in the manner directed by Act of Parliament.

*Given under my hand at Fort Townshend
St. John's, Newfoundland the 12th August 1822.*

Hamilton

*By His Excellency's Command
Signed P.C. Le Gayt*

Me (triumphantly): "Well Mr. Shea, what do you say to that? It's clear and definite. It's honest. I'm sure that not one of your members of the House knows of this document. It's bound to have been eaten by the rats, deliberately forgotten in the pigeon holes of your registry!"

My Friend: "Has this proclamation *ever been revoked?*"

Me: "I rather ask if it has *ever been obeyed.* Today, if a governor dared adopt such a tone, a revolution would explode immediately, both inside and outside the Colonial Parliament. This is how the Newfoundlanders practice the spirit of justice and honesty!"

Mr. Shea (humiliated but sincere): "You're right!"

Me: "Ah! I only have the last paragraph left to read to you. Mr. Shea, are you too overcome?"

Mr. Shea (smiling): "No. Let there be light!"

Me: "Yes, it's about time your island was taken out of the fog." I'll go on:

The proclamation of Governor Hamilton didn't discourage the Newfoundland Colonists. They approached London by a petition to the Colonial Office and made their grievances resound through Parliament. A member, named Robinson, warmly espoused their cause and for several years rose in his place to denounce the negligence of the Governor towards the colony. "It is strange," said he in 1835, "that after 21 years of peace, the people of Newfoundland do not yet know if they have a concurrent right with the French *to fish on their own coasts.* I protest against any delay in so grave a matter. The only rights of the French *are those coming to them from the treaty of Utrecht.*"

The English Cabinet refused to reply, knowing very well that no useful debate could be held on this point, and Mr. Robinson wasted his eloquence and his erroneous assertions. These attacks were renewed in the years following without affecting the relations of the two great powers. They had, nonetheless, one effect, which was to demonstrate to France that her rights needed confirmation to avoid her being cheated. An approach was therefore made by the French diplomats to lead the London Cabinet to recognize the *exclusive right* by a formal declaration. But the English Minister feared to furnish ammunition to the opposition or to provoke a storm in the Colony of Newfoundland, and was long deaf to the overtures. Finally his hesitations gave way under the influence of the friendly relations created by the two countries by a brotherhood in arms and the victories of the Crimea. The plenipotentiaries of the two governments came to an agreement in 1857 on a convention which gave recognition to exclusive French fishery rights and shore rights:

(1) In the East, from Cape St. John to Quirpon Island.
(2) In the North, from Quirpon Island to Cape Norman.
(3) In the West, from Cape Norman to Point Roche in Bay of Islands as well as in five other specially designated harbours.

The events which followed will be remembered. At the news of this convention a veritable mutiny exploded in the capital of Newfoundland. A furious multitude raced through the streets roaring against the Queen's Government and trailing the Royal Arms at the tail of a horse.

My friend (indignantly): "Oh!!!"

Mr. Shea shifted his position, feeling that his dignity demanded a protest. "Why, such a thing is inconceivable."

Me (pitilessly): "It is a felonious act that all the blood spilled by seals and codfish will never serve to wash away." I concluded:

"It was under the auspices of a rather doubtful good faith that the Anglo French treaty was submitted for the approval of the Colonial legislature. It goes without saying that it was rejected with one voice. The treaty remained unratified.

"The convention of 1857, in spite of being aborted, nonetheless remains a precious document on the fishery question, for it bears witness that England, by the voice of its Government and its official negotiators, has recognized the French claims as well-founded. This episode placed British diplomacy in a very embarrassing situation; for the absence of the Royal signature does not vitiate the agreements made in the sessions where the English plenipotentiaries admitted the title and ratified the regime instituted by France 85 years ago.

"*Contra renuntiatum non est regressus.*" It is impossible for them today to cite the treaty of Utrecht and the first treaty of Versailles.[22]

Mr. Shea: "This brochure is well got up. I'm astonished at not having seen it sooner. Could you leave it with me?"

Me: "Indeed, yes. But I'd like it to be conscientiously meditated on by all the good people of Newfoundland. In this way perhaps no one would dare to teach in Newfoundland schools that 'at the present time a part of our coast is virtually alienated from the control of the Colonial Government because of the ill-founded claims sustained and asserted by the French, in virtue of which these parts of the coast are generally, but very wrongly, called the French Shore'."[23]

Just then someone knocked.

Mr. Shea: "Come in."

Me (to my friend): "The Prime Minister! How do you do, sir?"

Sir William Whiteway (wishing to appear gracious): "Ah! How do you do?"

Mr. Shea. (presenting my friend): "Sir William, Mr. –.

(Sir William excuses himself and takes Mr. Shea aside for a few moments. Then he bows and goes out.)

Me: "He interrupted me just as I was going to speak of him."

My friend: "His face doesn't attract me. What man is that?"

Me: "Everyone, except a gentleman. Did you notice his ape-like paw?"

Mr. Shea: "Oh, you're going to give this gentleman a very poor idea of us."

Me: "It's often good to tear the mask from people who make use of it to act dishonestly. Besides, one has only to open the first number of the *Evening Telegram* that comes to hand and one is sure to encounter the name of Whiteway embellished with the most excoriating of epithets. Myself, I am content to judge what he is. It matters little to me on what path he seeks to lead his country. What I reproach in him is that he has, by his dishonesty, made any definite arrangement about the fisheries impossible."

Mr. Shea: "How so?"

Me: "You know as well as I do, but I'll explain it to my friend.

"Some years ago a conference assembled in London to deal with the question of our fishery rights in Newfoundland. Mr. Whiteway was invited as the Colony's representative. Naturally he went to any lengths to render any understanding impossible; but he came back with everything he coveted! The Cross of St. Michael and St. George, an order created for the Colonies and which gave him the title of 'Sir.' When he could write "Sir William Whiteway K.C.M.G." he believed himself a great man and his ambition knew no limits. Coming up from nothing, he had no scruple either of blood or breeding. Besides, he was a Scot. All means seemed good to him and the best, to start with, was to lie. 'Lie, keep on lying, and you'll always make a profit.'

"Sir William took this phrase as a rule of conduct; sprung from the common people, he had first coveted distinction. Now that the way was open to him, in his poverty he was avid of riches. He was Attorney General and a member of the House. By dint of speaking, he ended by making himself heard: by dint of lying, he made himself believed. He persuaded the voters that he had settled their business in London, that it was thanks to him that their legitimate aspirations had been satisfied. Henceforth, they could fish where they liked and erect fishing stations on any part of the coast they pleased. He claimed also to have obtained authority to name magistrates on the French Shore.

WILLIAM WHITEWAY. "All means seemed good to him and the best, to start with, was to lie. 'Lie, keep on lying and you'll always make a profit.'"

"He carried his impudence so far as to have all these lies printed and posted up in the form of a proclamation in all the villages of his electoral district. They believed him implicitly. The good folk of Newfoundland were too happy about it to seek to clarify it. What a man.

"He had then succeeded where so many diplomats of genius had failed for a century.

The lion was once more vanquished by the mouse. Newfoundland had humiliated France and Sir William was re-elected and became Prime Minister. 'Lie, keep on lying and you'll always make a profit.'

"But alas! It sometimes happens that Truth gets weary of the depths of her well and may be surprised, all naked, on the margin of it. As she is a ravishing beauty all those who discover her thus, be it our French seamen or the political enemies of Mr. Whiteway, are moved to call a crowd around to contemplate her. Many a blind man has been enlightened by her. The elections have clearly shown this in the last session. Do you believe, Mr. Shea, that Sir William would have been elected without the well-known influence of your brother?"

Mr. Shea: "Perhaps. I know that he put a lot of work into it."

Me: "And that he splashed around as much of your money as he could.

"Believe me, it's becoming evident that it's not a great minister, but a great humbug who directs the politics of Newfoundland. It's only because of self-interest that some seem still to be loyal to him—and even these only among those in political jobs.

"Now Mr. Whiteway rose by the common people and he will fall by the common people. You can imagine the indignant surprise of a poor Newfoundland fisherman who, on the faith of declarations by Whiteway, has come calmly to exercise his industry in our waters, when our warships steam up and order him to go away. They tell him he is breaking the law. 'But,' says he, 'they have posted a notice at home, a notice by Sir William Whiteway in which it says –etc.' They tell him, it is false and that he has been deceived. How can that be? They show him nothing in writing and what he saw was in print. However, he is forced to go away. His voyage, his family's only means of living, is spoiled because of the time lost in changing stations and he must arrive at this infallible conclusion—either the French are chasing me away without the right to do it and I'll be revenged for it; or Mr. Whiteway has been fooling me and is a wretch whom I should hate because he's exploited me at the risk of my dying of hunger.

My friend: "But don't you think these poor people generally believe that the fault is on our side?"

Me: "Doubtless they started with that opinion, but when they see France keeping warships on their coasts at great cost purely for the purpose of enforcing the law on them, you'll find that they are no more stupid than other people and they will say to themselves, 'It can't be possible that a great nation like that would come here to cheat us right in the face of the English war vessels, if they were not right in their claims. Then it's Whiteway who's codding us!' Ah, if the great man could only be wrapped up in a sealskin, how many poor men would be delighted to skin him alive.

Mr. Shea: "Really, you are shocking. Let's leave Mr. Whiteway alone for a moment. It's my turn to overwhelm you, for with all impartiality, we have real wrongs to complain of."

Me: "I agree and we will listen to you."

My friend (mockingly): "That's that, rest a while, you must be exhausted. You've delivered a regular political harangue. You should run as a candidate against Mr. Whiteway. Except for naturalization, which you must obtain, you embody already all the requirements for eligibility."

Me: "I've opened up pretty quickly the question of the French Shore."

Mr. Shea: "Perhaps. Do you really know what we are asking for? First, whatever you do or say, you will always be thought of here as trespassers. I know very well that this epithet shocks you and that you reproach us bitterly for it. Just imagine that the Normandy coast could only be fished by Americans. With what eye would you watch these people come every year to chase you away and take your places. They might well have their papers in order. You would not the less consider them as…"

Me: "But, my dear sir, we are our own masters for 15 centuries and Newfoundland is only yours since yesterday: It is we who discovered its fisheries. It is we who made it a country; it belonged to us for a long time and it's only due to M. de Vergennes that we possess it no longer. If you have a property, isn't it permissible to you to sell it subject to a reservation? We could have taken everything by the treaty of Versailles and we contented ourselves with the fishing rights.

"You should at least be civil to us and indeed be infinitely grateful to us for not keeping everything, because if you were under French rule you would not have the precious liberty which you now enjoy. If you had trailed *our* banner in the mud we would have sent you cannon shot instead of a constitution."

Mr. Shea: "Say what you like, it's none the less irritating for Newfoundlanders not to be masters in Newfoundland. Do they think they can stop us from developing our mines? We have some very rich ones which would be the source of an immense revenue for the Colony. But because they are on the French Shore we can do nothing in the matter."

My friend: "What do you mean by the French Shore?"

Mr. Shea: "It's those parts of the coast on which the French exercise certain fishing rights arising from treaties."

Me: "Yes, and this eloquent circumlocution is the one used officially to designate the French Shore for this term which means 'Virage Francais' sounds unpleasantly like sarcasm in Newfoundland ears."

FRENCH ROOMS AT ST. JULIAN HARBOUR. "We are our own masters for fifteen centuries and Newfoundland is only your since yesterday. It is we who discovered its fisheries. It is we who made it a country."

My friend: "So be it, but I didn't quite grasp why we prevent you from developing your mines. Surely they are not all absolutely on the waterline?"

Mr. Shea: "No, but we have no way out except by sea, so that we find ourselves unable to ship out our minerals because we are not allowed to land on this part of the Island nor to erect the facilities necessary to the functioning of this industry. This is one of the main reasons which made us undertake the railway lines that are now in sight of being built."

Me: "Yes, but don't count on our peacefully allowing you to drive your railheads right on to our territory."

Mr. Shea (smiling): "Oh, I'm sure you will protest, as you have done every time we have appointed magistrates to the French Shore. But you know better than I that that doesn't bother us very much: the Government sends a simple acknowledgement to the Consul and everything ends there!"

Me: "Yes, but we've done enough for politeness. With people like you, a delicate approach is useless. You are pretty shrewd. You make an advance and if sometimes you are forced to retreat, you never go back where you started from. It is forbidden to you by the treaties to have any permanent buildings on the coasts reserved to us. You have gone so far as to build there little towns and villages. Today you push your insolence so far as the stationing of magistrates, which is an official recognition of the existence of these villages, which are there in contravention of the law, and then, because we seem to close our eyes to this instead of protesting, you now dare to complain that our seamen are smuggling into these settlements. But they are not smuggling since these towns are not officially in existence."

Mr. Shea: "You can't deny that they do it at sea when our fishermen go to sell them bait."

Me: "That's another matter. I agree they do it and so much the worse for you. You understand…"

My friend: "What is 'bait'?"

Me: "Oh, that's right, 'bait' is the lure they use to fish for cod. It consists of types of fish they find here on the coast, so that the Newfoundland fishermen are supplied with them when ours arrive. So they go to meet them at sea and sell them bait in return for rum and other commodities that are subject to high customs duties. Naturally the Customs suffer from it, but one must confess that our seamen would be silly to have any scruples in this matter considering that this immediate supply puts them in a position to commence their fishing sooner.

"So, my dear sir, here are all your wrongs. Not being entirely free in your own country, being unable to develop your mines nor end your railways on our coasts, to be crossed in the matter of your magistrates and cheated by our smugglers! Is there anything else?"

Mr. Shea: "No, that's all."

Me: "Well, I'm sure we can come to an understanding between us."

Mr. Shea (smiling): "Well then, your Excellency, what do you propose?"

FRENCH ROOMS AT CAPE ROUGE HARBOUR. "It is forbidden to you by the treaties to have any permanent buildings on the coasts reserved to us. You have gone so far as to build there little towns and villages."

Me: "First, what do the treaties say? They give us French the exclusive right of fishing on that part of the coast between Cape St. John on the east coast and Cape Rouge on the west, passing around by the north. The enjoyment of this right is given us from April 5th to October 5th. In addition we can cut all the wood we need on the coast for flakes to dry our fish. Our fishermen pay no customs duties on the French Shore.

"You English are forbidden to fish on the part of the coast reserved to us. You have even less right to put up shore establishments as no settlement is permissible. Neither magistrates nor other officials can exist. This absolute prohibition on your establishing anything on the French Shore prevents you at the same time from developing your mines and from finishing your railway. This being established, and you must have the good faith to recognize the truth of these principles, I would say to you: develop your mines freely. We will give up to you for this purpose any point on the French Shore that you will designate as being most convenient to you as a loading port.

"Organize on our coasts whatever administration you please; have members of parliament appoint magistrates. Install *there* a Customs office and police. Only we reserve for our seamen free entry for everything they bring in to serve the purposes of their industry; and we would authorize you to have them watched by your police and proceeded against in case of frauds.

"As for your railway, run it where you like.

"In exchange for so many concessions in your favour and so valuable to you, and which we think we owe you in equity and out of regard for liberty, we expect you to cause our rights to be respected with the most scrupulous exactitude.

"To help you in this responsibility, we ask that the officers of our naval stations be given the same powers of suppressing breaches of the law as have those of the English stations; and we expect that when an action is taken for an offence committed by one of your nationals, you will not content yourselves with a simple and illusory acknowledgement of its reception. We wish that the matter be brought immediately before your courts and that the guilty be punished as they deserve.

"As for bait, as you can't stop the traffic, you can do no better than allow your fishermen to bring it to ours."

Mr. Shea (seriously, after a moment of reflection): "Yes. I think that under these conditions we could come to an understanding. Only it's that diabolical exclusive right that is shocking to us. It seems to me that you could easily let our fishermen go into the bays that yours leave unoccupied, with an obligation that they would go away when yours arrived."

Me: "Most certainly! A cat would have plenty of space in a room with a rat, but that wouldn't stop her eating it. This mixing of your fishermen with ours would be the cause of continuous quarrels. You must know that there would be few conscientious enough to go away, as you say, without protesting or even without resisting. It's precisely to avoid so many undesirable complications that we have done everything to assure that our fishery rights will be exclusive. Remember the attempt that was made to implement the combination you spoke of. At the end of very few years both England and France very soon agreed in recognizing the impossibility of this *modus vivendi* and wiped it out of existence.

"After all, you have a stretch of coast more than sufficient to employ all your fishermen; and remember that in exchange for the tranquility that we ask you to assure to our people, we undertake to recognize officially the political existence of Newfoundland on the French Shore. There is nothing more precious that you can gain."

Mr. Shea (gravely): "Indeed, all that could be arranged to the satisfaction of both parties; but you can be sure of one thing, that no satisfactory result will ever be achieved while France tries to deal directly with England in this matter. She should come to an agreement with us first, since the sanction of Parliament is essential to any treaty she can conclude with the British Government. You can rest content that England will not force us at gunpoint to accept an arrangement secretly arrived at with France. She can't declare war on us and, in frustrating us, she's very afraid she might drive us to revolt and see us escape from her sovereignty.

"Did not somebody knock?"

GUARDIANS OF A FISHING ROOM AND HIS FAMILY, JACQUES CARTIER ISLAND.
"This mixing of your fishermen with ours would be the cause of continuous quarrels. You must know that there would be few conscientious enough to go away, as you say, without protesting or resisting."

My friend: "I think so."

Mr. Shea: "Come in."

A voice: "The Council is awaiting Your Honour to convene."

Mr.Shea: "Gentlemen, you will excuse me? I must..."

My friend: "Of course, sir, but we are very grateful to you for granting so long an interview."

Me: "Three hours! What have we done! And what do you think of the Colonial Secretary?"

My friend: "Charming. And he's a man of character who breathes good faith and since we have seen the Premier at the Colonial Secretary's, there's no point in going again to interview him in his office."

We went out of the building and went back to the lower town. At the Queen's wharf just in front of the Custom House, the boat master of the *Clorinda* was waiting for any officers who wanted to go back aboard.

The *Clorinda* is an old, high-masted frigate in which they had installed a feeble steam engine. She is commanded by a captain who is the supreme authority over our Newfoundland Naval Squadron. He has three other ships under his command—two sailing schooners and a mixed transport, the *Indre*. On the other side, the English squadron consists of three steam cruisers of the third and fourth grade, and far more suitable for the service required for coastal patrol. There are indeed many bays whose mouths are too narrow to allow passage to a ship like the *Clorinda*, and thereby allow the Newfoundlanders to fish with impunity under the very eyes of the French. Only our schooners can penetrate these narrows. But as they have no steam it's not unusual for a contrary wind to hold them in sight of the delinquents, but impotent to reach them.

The Commander of the squadron has many times complained of this state of affairs and finally it was decided to meet his demands by replacing the two schooners with a ram-gunboat of a new fast type.

Today we have three steamboats in Newfoundland waters, as have the English, but at the time I am writing of in St. John's, we are only at the beginning of 1883. The *Canadienne* and the *Evangeline* continued to tack about the length of the French Shore while the three English craft, screw driven, went straight to their objectives. The biggest of them, the *Tenedos*, is under the orders of a captain who has the title of Senior Commander of the English Squadron but who, instead of reporting directly to the Admiralty, as does our commander, is responsible to the Vice-Admiral commanding the West Indies fleet and the British North American Provinces, whose residence is at Halifax.

Following this explanation of the relative state of the French and English war-ships cruising in Newfoundland, we will return to the French Shore question and tell what is the mission of these ships and how they carry it out.

Each year, when the drifting of the ice allows free access to the Newfoundland coasts, the schooners both French and native, hasten towards the places frequented by the cod. Ours go to the French Shore and the natives take over the bays on the rest of the coast. Does this really happen? Not in the least. If everyone kept his own place there would be no need for police. But, as we know already, one side asserts their exclusive right to a given part of the territory, and the other side denies it. From this comes invasion of the first by the second—brawls, fists and complications of all sorts.

Then England and France, agreed in their good will to keep the peace between their fishermen, send in their warships, instructed to exercise on the spot the high functions of an international police and to inspire at the same time a salutary fear in the poor deluded electors of Mr. Whiteway.

However, aboard each English ship, one of the officers has been invested by the Colonial Government with the powers of a Justice of the Peace and can inflict penalties on the delinquents, while the French have only the ineffective right of making a formal protest.

If a Newfoundland schooner is surprised by one of our cruisers in the fishing areas reserved to us, she is ordered to go away. If she refuses, she is stripped of her fishing gear and a complaint against her is sent by the French Commander to the English Commander. The latter responds by a simple acknowledgement and makes an investigation which, for fear of the Colonial Government, always ends up by establishing the innocence of the guilty—or does not end up at all; and the malicious fisherman, who knows the trick, goes back again at the first opportunity.

It therefore occurs that, in the final result, the surveillance of our ships is purely illusory, but it serves at least to affirm the strong basis on which our rights are founded.

Justly alarmed for the future of our fisheries by the futility of the results obtained, and wishing at all costs to render them more fruitful by forcing the issue, the Commander and the French Consul joined forces to conclude the business by direct action towards the Queen's Governor. Up to then, the complaint set up by the French Commander was sent to the English Commander. The latter made an enquiry and then sent a report on the matter to the Governor. At the end of the season, all these items form a file which is then sent to the Foreign Office, where doubtless they never have time to read them.

Without question, this system must be changed. Our fishermen are sick of difficulties being created on the French Shore. In the last 20 years, the number of our schooners has diminished on the grounds to an alarming extent. Every day, the Newfoundlanders grow more arrogant because of their impunity, and take no notice of treaties. They simply repudiate them. According to them, the treaties do not give us an exclusive right but only the right of fishing without competition; and it was not competition, they said, to occupy our bays when we had not occupied them first. Our status, already compromised, threatened to be altogether lost.

We needed to assert our rights at the top of our voices as quickly as possible so as to appear to be giving concessions, not giving-in to force. This happy understanding, which existed for the first time between the agent for foreign affairs (the Consul) and the Navy, gave hope of more success. It nonetheless came to nothing through the inertia of the Governor who got out of it by a simple acknowledgement, adding that he would acquaint the Colonial Government with the matter. And the wheel went round as usual.

I'll stop for a moment; perhaps I'm saying too much of things that have so far received no publicity. Besides, what use to bring up again something so ancient which for 50 years has called forth conferences as futile as they were numerous?

The latest, made up of plenipotentiaries both English and French, assembled in Paris in February 1884. Naturally they broke up without coming to any understanding.

However, the same plenipotentiaries were called together again in the following April. France and England finished by coming to complete agreement and drafting a treaty, but this latter could have no validity until ratified by the Newfoundland Government and the ratification hasn't come yet. For, sacrificing as always to the sacred routine, in place of first seeking to deal with Newfoundland, and later consulting England—the only way of getting real results—the French Government pretended to embrace, as always, every possible chance of failure.

Is there something superhuman, then, in the vanity that the Newfoundlanders hold in their hearts, that it is so hard to understand it and make use of it? Isn't it quite natural that a small country that has the power to say 'no' should say it, if only to show that it can defy with impunity two great nations? We must then go first to her (Newfoundland) and flatter her by a direct approach. We must recognize all she has taken with a pretence of having given it all in a pure spirit of benevolence, and then offer some small enticement as a last argument in consideration of the nearness of the United States. Then one will have made considerable progress.

Old England would be only too happy to confirm! But, of course, we must continue in the traditional mistakes: And the Republic, by love of tradition, rushes into a new diplomatic failure, ideally designed to show the Newfoundlanders their strength and encourage them to be all the more demanding. Then they will inundate the Governor with more and more indignant protests, to which he will certainly be polite enough to reply with a banal acknowledgement delicately tied up in blue ribbon.

FRENCH FISHING BOAT. "Isn't it quite natural that a small country that has the power to say 'no' should say it, if only to show that it can defy with impunity two great nations?"

But whistles are sounding on the frigate's deck, a voice cries orders, and a squad is lined up with grounded arms. The Commander's whale-boat is coming alongside. Here he is; they present arms! He is already an old acquaintance, so let us profit by his invitation to visit him in his quarters. We go under the poop and go through the dining room into the lounge. It is spacious, comfortable, with red settees along the partitions and stern windows with two sashes opening on a gallery.

"Read that!" he said to us, holding out a newspaper. It was the *Evening Mercury,* the official organ of the Colonial Government. When I had given him back the sheet:

"You will remember well what happened, you've read the many English and French reports which have been issued on the matter and which can be summed up as follows:

"In a bay on the French Shore, already occupied by one of our fisherman, three Newfoundland fishermen came to fish for cod. The Frenchman unsuccessfully asked them to go away. The English nationals commenced their preparations for fishing. Then the French skipper decided to oppose them by stripping them of their gear and the rigging of their ships. His purpose, in this last measure, was to make the delinquents incapable of flight while he sent a party to seek a warship, French or English, as witness to the offence. He succeeded in this plan but not without getting a broken head from one of the English skippers who, seeing himself taken, hit him brutally over the head with a gaff.

"A warship came up after a few days and a careful enquiry was made. The Newfoundland skipper accepted the blame. Besides, he was in default for having a schooner with no name on her stern. In his turn, the English captain examined the evidence and again the native confessed his faults, but all this translated into English means that the Newfoundlander was innocent as a new-born babe and the Frenchman never got a crack on the head."

"Yes, Commander, for anyone reading only the article in the *Evening Mercury* no other opinion would be possible." The conclusion is that there is no hope of obtaining justice against these raiders and forcing them to respect our rights.

The adventure of the *Canadienne* was no way surprising. One day the armed schooner in question came upon a flotilla of Newfoundland fishing boats installed in one of our bays. In vain she tried to expel them in the name of the treaties. The delinquents were unimpressed by the size of the schooner and thought up a thousand excuses for not going, so much so that the commander of the *Canadienne* ended the argument by letting his guns talk for him. The cod went out and after them went their brethren of the coast. One can easily form an idea of what is needed in tact, energy and moderation in the naval captain who, usually for a three year term, is the commander of the Newfoundland squadron.

The *Clorinda* arrives in June and goes home at the end of September. All this time is spent in patrolling the French Shore. She scarcely wets her anchor in the port of St. John's. This year she began her inspection in the North and only put into anchorage at the end of June. She is now ready to return to the French fishing grounds and, while waiting for her to come back to say good-bye, I will again submerge myself in Newfoundland life and study their mode of living.

A three-year-old cod, white and fat, of which the flesh comes away in soft and savoury flakes, is the eternally remembered regret of those who have been in Newfoundland.

7

THE JUDICIARY, QUIDI VIDI AND COD

J ULY 2nd—Yesterday was Sunday and I dined at the Bishop's where my table companion was a judge, a charming man with a caustic verve and a contempt for the Islanders. 'Savages' he called them. While they were discussing the missions and praising the faith and virtue of the Newfoundlanders, I whispered to my companion. "Are all these fine fellows as perfect before human justice as we can believe them to be before God's?"

"Sir, in the year of grace 1833,[24] only the other day, in the address at the opening of the Supreme Court, the Chief Justice pronounced the memorable words: 'Gentlemen, I am proud and happy to state that no offence or crime relating to your jurisdiction has been committed in the course of this year.'

"In the year I quote these words, times have certainly changed. The Golden Age didn't last long in any country; why should we expect it to be different in Newfoundland? The admission is difficult, but here it is all the same. Religion, which at first succeeded in maintaining a high degree of morality in the ruder classes of Newfoundland, later became the cause of the first crimes.

"Towards the end of September of this year of 1883, St. John's learned with fear and indignation that in a neighbouring settlement, a religious quarrel between Orangemen and Catholics had had a fatal termination. Alas, unreasoning faith engenders fanaticism. This knife-thrust was but the signal for greater disorders. The following year gave the gentlemen of the court plenty of business. This time it was the whole population of a Protestant town that rose against their Catholic neighbours. The police no longer had authority. The riot became a religious war. Help had to be asked from the Crown. The *Tenedos*, the cruiser commanding the Newfoundland squadron, was sent from Halifax to restore order.

"But the St. John's people were cruelly hurt in their self-esteem. What a humiliation to have to beg for help from English soldiers, when they had already demanded and obtained the evacuation of the English garrison. And remember that up to now, nobody barred their door in the evening or went armed when travelling at night, because nobody feared either robbers or highwaymen.

"The Supreme Court had nothing to do. Its judges pocketed fat salaries for doing nothing. It seemed a pity that a magistracy so well organized should find itself abandoned by the criminal world. Now they have blown the ancient dust from their law books and are finding a use for their first wig."

After stopping a moment to smile and let his phrase produce its full effect, Judge Carlston[25] said: "I'm only speaking, of course, of the Supreme Court. That which was created in 1826 by promulgation of a Royal Charter. It is composed of a Chief Justice and two assistant judges named by the Crown. The Chief Justice ranks immediately after the Governor. It is he who fills the post of Administrator of the Government of the Colony and that of Judge of the Vice-Admiralty Court when these posts are vacant."

"The Supreme Court sits twice a year at St. John's and also goes on circuit on the island at times and places fixed by the Governor. The salary of the Chief Justice is $5000 a year, and that of the assistant judges is $4000. There are also two other courts, that of Labrador, which has a civil and criminal jurisdiction on all that part of Labrador that is subject to Newfoundland, and the Central District Court which sits, when there is need, in St. John's to deal with the civil cases of the district. Its two judges are named by the Governor-in-Council and each gets $2000. Finally, there is a Sheriff for each judicial district on the island. The foregoing should make you familiar with the system. No, not quite, for the beauty of all this is that our salary is for life. When we have retired, our salaries continue to be issued to us as if we were on the active list."

Just then we were interrupted by one of the guests who, at the request of the Bishop, started up a song. Several others did the same one after another to the great delight of His Lordship. One of them distinguished himself gracefully in singing in an agreeable voice "The Hills of the Pyrenees." It was Father Galveston, an old friend, a priest of the Cathedral and an artist who spoke both French and Italian. After dinner I congratulated him and we arranged a meeting for next day to take a walk together.

I have just left him (We had been to the Village of Quidi Vidi). Nothing could be more romantic than this nest of fishermen. First one strolls along the shore of Quidi Vidi lake for its full length; and at its end one crosses a torrent that hardly has time to murmur a short song before it disappears in salt water.

At first sight it seems that it is throwing itself into a second lake before achieving an even more violent escape. Not at all. It's the sea; it's a chasm; it's a tomb. But what a lovely tomb. The ocean, which penetrates into this tiny cove by one knows not what invisible opening, lingers on the breast of the rock, calm and limpid as the water of a spring. On the right are platforms of dead branches where cod are drying. They lean over the water on their wooden stilts.

QUIDI VIDI VILLAGE. "We have been to the Village of Quidi Vidi. Nothing could be more romantic than this nest of fishermen."

Ten or 12 little fishermen's dwellings—all the village—rear in the background, with clean white walls and slate roofs. They press against the bottom of the cliffs, which are covered in a thick layer of plants and shrubs that flower with all the colours of the rainbow. Higher up, the naked rock is scored with vivid scars. In the middle, at the bottom, on the white and blue water, a boat throws a black shadow that glides silently to the shore where she goes to land the fruit of her fishing; and always one asks oneself, where is this vast and invisible ocean from which comes this little boat which a rock is sufficient to hide? To reach it, one must go around the cliff and one does not perceive the green and treacherous wave until it carries one away.

Quidi Vidi! A strange name, both poetic and barbarous. Father Galveston, who sought frantically to establish the etymology and origin of the name, or less extravagant place names of his island, repeated in despair this name, wild as the note of a bird. I learned since that he has found a meaning in the Breton dialect.

A faint whiff of codfish changed the theme of our conversation. The cod! This fish is so delicious, so delicate, so tasty. I could almost say it is the best of all fishes and still so often slandered! A three-year-old cod, white and fat, of which the flesh comes away in soft and savoury flakes, is the eternally remembered regret of those who have been in Newfoundland and who can never find, in any other place, such a gastronomic experience of which they now can retain only the exquisite memory. It is true that the odour rising from the shores of Quidi Vidi comes from sun-dried cod, and I admit that in that condition this noble fish is much less seductive.

As the boat approached, we waited to help with the unloading and the dressing of the fish. When the boat stopped, the dory, lashed to her stern, was brought up alongside and the catch was landed and brought to the fisherman's stage. There, on the splitting table, with the aid of a stiff and pointed knife, the fish is cut up, gutted, split in two and boned. The liver is separated first, placed in a tub and set aside to make oil. The head and the entrails are set apart and destined to be sold to farmers for fertilizer. Finally the tongue, also saved, makes a delicate tit-bit, although a little too gelatinous. Thus amputated, the cod passes to the hands of a second operator who splits it lengthwise along the spine and takes out the bone.

The salter then starts his work; washes off the last traces of blood, sprinkles the fish with a handful of coarse salt and piles it up on the floor. At the end of a certain time, the heap is separated, the fish is washed and spread on flakes to dry in the sun.

The "flake" is a platform of small rails covered with fir branches and raised on stakes so that the air can circulate freely underneath. A man with a sort of fork sticks the fish and passes it to those who wait on the flakes. It is then essential to give it the greatest care. If it rains, or on the contrary if the sun is too hot, it is placed again in piles. The most favourable atmospheric conditions are a medium temperature and a sky with frequent clouds. Well dried, the fish

THE NEWFOUNDLAND COD FISHERIES. "There, on the splitting table, with the aid of a stiff and pointed knife, the fish is cut up, gutted, split in two and boned."

are brought to the wharf of the merchants who divide it into four grades of quality. There are about 40 fish to a quintal and a quintal is worth, on an average, about four dollars or 21 francs, 60 centimes.

The cod fishery is carried out in three different areas: on the Banks of Newfoundland, on the coasts of the island of that name and on a part of Labrador. The Grand Bank, lying to the east of the island in mid ocean, is 600 miles long and 300 broad. It is the veritable fatherland, the home of the cod. There they abound in inexhaustible quantities, and man destroys very little in comparison with the carnage caused by all sorts of marine monsters.

In spite of all, it is impossible to admit that the number of cod is diminishing. In the nearly 400 years that they have been sought in these waters, they continue to appear in abundance, and already this year's fishery appears to be more rewarding than ever.

The Bank fishery is followed almost exclusively by the French and a little by the United States. It's a hard profession, that of the men who drop anchor in open sea, men who are hardy enough to station themselves between heaven and earth out of sight of any shore. In that place, a cold 'norther' pitilessly shakes the boat, an old brig or three-master, which rises and falls with groaning timbers, incapable of fleeing before the enemy.

Every morning the small boats, manned by three or four men, leave to seek the fish. But how often do they go never to return, or at least, to come to grief on some naked rock? I have seen these brave sailors, barred by the fog from returning to their ship. They had fought the sea to the death in their frail cockleshell, fought against fatigue, against cold and hunger, until good fortune had put them in the track of the schooner or the steamer that had picked them up. Then they go to the Consulate. Most of the time they are Bretons or Normans who speak an unintelligible French. Only, alas, their tattered clothes and torn hands speak with eloquence enough. Then they are given money for food, they are clothed and lodged until an opportunity occurs to repatriate them or help them regain ship. But some never come back.

When in 1713, abandoning Newfoundland to the English, France reserved the fishery rights on a part of the coast of the Island and on the Banks, she considered that these dangerous and fatiguing expeditions after the cod were a marvellous apprenticeship for the sailors who could afterwards be recruited for the Navy. In all the treaties anterior to that of Utrecht, France always showed herself careful to safeguard these rights, for whose conservation she is still fighting today.

Every year in April, the French ships arrive in St. Pierre-Miquelon. There they land the merchandise of all kinds that they have brought from the Mainland for the traders of our Colony. Then they provide themselves with bait and leave for the fishery. The bait, namely the lure for taking the cod, varies according to the season.

The first voyage, in June and July, which is usually the most fruitful, is made with caplin. It is a little white fish, very like a sardine, which in early summer swarms on the Newfoundland coast in such abundance that they are taken in cartloads and used as much for manure to enrich the soil as for bait for the cod. At the end of six or seven weeks, the caplin disappears after spawning. Its place is soon taken by the squid. They are fished from mid-July to the end of August, and when they

OFF FOR THE BANKS. "It's a hard profession, that of the men who drop anchor in open sea, men who are hardy enough to station themselves between heaven and earth out of sight of any shore."

commence to disappear, legions of herring blockade the island until winter. This last fish makes a very tasty dish, and it is sent in great quantities to Canada and the United States, preserved in ice.

Our banking fleet sails, at first provided with caplin. When this bait is used, they return to St. Pierre to land the products of their voyage with their dealers. The cod, already salted, is put to dry on land. Then they must stock up with squid and sail again. At the end of August they return to land this second catch, which is handled like the first. Lastly, loaded with herring, the ships set sail for a third and last voyage. But this time instead of bringing their load back to St. Pierre they take, without detour, the way to France loaded with "green cod," as they call the fish which is salted but not dried.

The hazards and risks run on the Banks are such for the suppliers that for a long time our fisheries fell into decline. A premium of ten francs per quintal of cod was then instituted by the Government. This measure saved us so well that the Newfoundlanders abandoned all competition and gave place to the French who are, at this time, almost the only operators.

Today, France catches from four to five hundred thousand quintals of cod per year on the Banks and coasts of Newfoundland. In 1871, this industry brought to the Mainland ten million five hundred francs; and in 1874 from fifteen to twenty million. As for the Newfoundlanders and English, they fish in schooners along a part of the island and part of Labrador. They have more than 50,000 boats employed in this industry.[26]

The cod is taken in many ways, by line, by seine, by net and by trap. The simplest way is by hook-and-line; but when the cod is glutted it won't bite (although ordinarily it is so voracious that often stones and pieces of iron are found in its stomach); then they use other means. The seine, used a lot by our fishermen, is a net from 100 to 120 fathoms long and from 50 to 100 feet deep in the centre, but narrowing towards the ends. This seine is thrown around a shoal of fish and pulled in, it is then hauled and contains, often, from 40 to 50 tons of fish.[27] They use also a line furnished with hundreds of hooks called a "bultow" by the Newfoundlanders. It is laid on the banks on the coasts, at the entry to the bays, and is left there all night, anchored and buoyed.

The annual combined catch of the French, the Newfoundlanders and the Americans is estimated to average 3,700,000 quintals of cod valued at 80,000,000 francs.

Normally, the cod is found in the Atlantic between 77° and 30° North latitude. They cannot live in the Gulf Stream because of the unduly high temperature of the water. On the contrary, they abound in the Arctic Current which bathes the Newfoundland coast. This brings with the icebergs quantities of mollusks and plankton embedded in the ice which form food for the herring and the herring form food for the cod.

Previously, a theory had been established on the migration of the herring and cod to the Arctic regions. Since then, observation has upset these ideas. It is known with certitude that they live always in the same place, but at spawning time they descend again and disappear in the depths where they were born. This, then, is this famous fish and this famous fishery which is the means of life for a whole people.[28]

If Newfoundlanders have penetrated the secret of being happy without paying taxes, I think they would find themselves no worse off under the authority of a municipality, and certainly the town would be much better off.

8

MUNICIPAL AFFAIRS AND THE RAILWAY

J ULY 16th—In truth, if I am no longer astonished by anything on the part of the young girls—not even by the flowers one of them sent me yesterday for my birthday—I find, in spite of myself, no causes for stupefaction. I've just come from the home of Dr. Galveston,[29] the priest's brother, where I was given a thousand details on the affairs of Newfoundland that I hasten to give here. But of all I have to say the most curious, the most ridiculous, the most unlikely for me, a Frenchman and a man from an advanced civilization, is the absence of direct taxes, municipal councils and a state registry.

DR. THOMAS HOWLEY. *"I've just come from the home of…the priest's brother, where I was given a thousand details on the affairs of Newfoundland that I hasten to give here."*

No direct taxes of any sort—what savages! The coffers of the treasury are filled exclusively by the customs duties augmented by some other insignificant revenues. It's true that importations—and everything is imported—are taxed exorbitantly.

However, if the Newfoundlanders have penetrated the secret of being happy without paying taxes, I think they would find themselves no worse off under the authority of a municipality, and certainly the town would be much better off. The streets are sewers; the sidewalks would break your neck. There is nothing to promote enjoyment in a walk or to please the eye. And still an atom of Tournay or a grain of Haussmann would only have to assist nature a little and promenaders would enjoy the most picturesque of meeting places. But they are too busy to think of that.

It's for the same reason, I suppose, that there is no state registry. What need? There is no military service, no compulsory school attendance. The act of baptism fills every need. Well, 50 years ago there was only one miserable carriage in all the Island of Newfoundland—it belonged to a doctor. Today there is a telephone in St. John's.

Here is something to baffle the city halls of the French Republic. Baffled! Why not, when we see so many marvelous discoveries made by our scientists, finding their practical application only in the New World? As for us, we wish to be skeptics in everything. The more a discovery is worth, the more we doubt its future. I'm afraid that this fine skepticism has become a mere habit.

The Americans may not have the time to think, but they know how to profit by what we discover for them. What country has made more advances in electric lighting than France? But we hardly use it, while in America it has become in many cases the indispensable means of illumination. While St. John's is an English town, it resembles in many respects her continental neighbours. It's true that there are neither theatres, nor public promenades, no music worthy of the name. It's true that the carriages are superannuated and the furnishings are in the most perfect bad taste. In a word, there is nothing for the sophisticate or the artist.

The people of Newfoundland are fishermen, its society are merchants and all the improvements relating to the fishery or to commerce are to be found in operation. You will find that this town, built of wood, has a dry dock just finished on a new plan, where the world's greatest ships can be received. Before leaving port, take a look at the rigging of the schooners. Their cables have been made in a ropewalk near St. John's and won a gold medal in 1833 at an international fishery exhibition in London.

Take care at night, in following the unpaved and scarcely lighted streets, of bumping against telephone poles. Avoid also those of the telegraph which spread across country and along roads that never see a roadman.

If you are driving, pay attention to the signposts of the railway. They will warn you that the rails cut across the road at this point. These are the only safeguards the company has provided. Otherwise, if you wish, you can walk the rails at your ease. Nothing prevents your access either in the country or in the streets of the town which it traverses between two houses. If you go along the line, you will finish by reaching a wooden shed. You may ask why the trains stop there! Why, because this is the station.

Don't think this railway is a laughing matter. Listen to its history. The first project was in 1875. Its author was the chief engineer of the Canadian Railways and had for its objective the creation of a more rapid travel route between England and America. He prepared a line of fast steamers carrying only mail, passengers, and express packages. These packets would come from Valentia in Ireland to St. John's, Newfoundland.

There they would disembark to cross the Island by rail to Bay St. George. A steamer service would be instituted between this point and Shippegan in Baie Chaleur from which a spur would go to join the Canadian and American network. Following this itinerary, the ocean crossing should not take more than four days and the whole trip from London to New York could be made in seven days.

In 1878, the project not having been carried out, Mr. Whiteway, feverish with ambition, resolved to push the affair, and with it his own fortunes in the legislature of the Colony. Beaten to his knees by powerful adversaries, he hoped to make himself popular by raising the cry of progress. He had plenty to do in this way, and to undertake it was to succeed. Once it was decided to make Newfoundland something more than a mere fishing station, it was essential to think of the means of attracting emigrants and of giving them a means of living. The fishermen might make their money by their trade; they were nonetheless miserable for part of the year, forced to idleness by the winter climate.

The building of a railway seemed a better expedient than any other to solve this problem. In fact, it would cross a wild country where there would be farmlands to cultivate and forests to develop. In the centre of the Island, the temperature is less severe. Agriculture would produce results at least in the raising of cattle. There are also mining lands which cannot be developed for lack of outlets. The Crown lands would be open to those who wished to settle and cultivate them.

In place of awaiting the needs of an established population, the railway is to be built first for the purpose of attracting settlement along its route. They expect that the whistle of the locomotive will be heard by thousands of emigrants and that, eventually, Newfoundland will become a real country like others. This is the general plan of the policy that has been called the "Policy of Progress," which is that of the present Government of Newfoundland.

To these seductive discourses, the "New Party" (enemies of Mr. Whiteway) replied by asserting that there were neither forests nor farmlands in the interior any more than on the coasts and that the venture would only serve to line the pockets of Mr. Whiteway and company. Only the future will decide and it is true, that if it is allowable to doubt the integrity of the Premier, his enemies from day to day seem to bring less warmth to their condemnations of him on this point. Mr. Whiteway then obtained from the Legislature an annual subsidy of $120,000 and liberal grants of Crown lands along the right-of-way for any company who would undertake the project of 1875.

But a difficulty arose that could easily have been anticipated with a little good faith. The Home Government refused its sanction because the line, ending in St. Georges, would find itself on the French Shore and that there were, at that moment, conversations going on with France on the subject of our fishing rights. After two years of vain waiting, Sir William Whiteway, not being able to build this line, proposed to construct another which would measure 340 miles and serve to develop the mines between Harbour Grace and Brigus.[30] He proposed to the Colony to undertake the work itself with finances that he claimed were adequate. A committee charged with the examination of the project made a favourable report which was adopted by the legislature. The enterprise was entrusted to an American firm. In return for an annual subvention of $180,000 and the grant of 5000 acres of farmland per mile of railway, it undertook to finish the line in five years. At the present time, there is a train service between St. John's and Harbour Grace, the two most important towns in Newfoundland.

In February 1882, during the session of the legislature, a demand was presented for a "Charter of Incorporation for the Great American and European Short-Line Railway Company." The plan of this company was to implement the idea of a great transportation line between America and England, passing through Newfoundland. The plan, better studied than the first, proposes to establish a first class railway from the east coast of Newfoundland to a point in the vicinity of Cape Ray, then a steamboat to take the mail and passengers to Cape North (Cape Breton), a distance of 56 miles. From there, a railway will go to the Strait of Canso. This crossing made, the network of Canadian and American Railroads is reached and travellers can proceed in all directions.

THE RAILWAY STATION AT FORT WILLIAM. "They expect that the whistle of the locomotive will be heard by thousands of emigrants and that, eventually, Newfoundland will become a real country like others."

A line of fast packets will be established between a port on the west coast of Ireland and the east coast of Newfoundland where the railway will begin. By this means, there would be two days less in going from London to New York than is needed today.

If things are really thus, all the great transatlantic companies will be forced to adopt this new route, and there is not the least doubt that Newfoundland will quickly feel the enormous advantage arising out of its position on the most frequented of ocean roads.

So the legislature hastened to adopt the new plan and the company, who took the responsibility, received in return the promise of 5000 acres of land per mile of railway, the right of exclusive use for 40 years and duty-free importation of all materials necessary for the construction and maintenance of the line.[31]

Here is something, not that I heard, but that I carefully checked in my conversation today. In spite of everything I think the politicians of Newfoundland have more ambition than capacity and that their country, in spite of their fine speeches in bad English, will never be anything but a fishing station unless some fine day the Americans lay their hand on it.[32]

Our songs sent French echoes sounding
through these solitudes where ordinarily the
only voice that murmurs is that of the sea
breeze which comes in the evening to wake
the sounds of the forest.

9

SALMONIER AND A FAREWELL

AUGUST 10th—Here we are, back in St. John's after the loveliest three day excursion that could be dreamed of. It had been arranged by Father Galveston and it was he who led the party. There were 10 of us, men and women. We went by rail to Holyrood, about two hours' journey, where we dined on the provisions that we all carried. Then we went by carriage across the isthmus which joins the peninsula of Avalon to the rest of the Island and thus arrived at Salmonier at the home of the parish priest of the place, Father St. John, who was expecting us.[33] The bell rang for the departure, the train got underway and, after crossing two or three streets, we saw the sea and did not lose sight of it again until our arrival, while on the other side was the wild country, silent and still.

But how can one paint in words the marvellous aspect of this countryside unknown to the whole world; the ravishing view that extends around the railway line between Topsail and

HOLYROOD. *"How can one paint in words the marvelous aspect of this countryside...the ravishing view that extends around the railway line between Topsail and Holyrood, the waves that for an hour of the journey rolled up and died along the rails?"*

Holyrood, the waves that for an hour of the journey rolled up and died along the rails, the horizon bounded by several rocky islands and by the farther silhouette of a coast with fantastic indentations, and the gentle harbour of Holyrood with the great dome-like rock that overhangs it; the improvised luncheon in the white inn where we had surprised two young honeymooners who had chosen this romantic nest so as to treasure a highly poetic memory of their first kisses: and the four hours of driving through a continuous virgin forest of hundred-year-old fir trees with white tops; the lakes spreading on all sides on which there extends in perfumed splendour the white flowers of the water lily with its heart of gold; the magnificent silence and desolate solitude of the wilderness only disturbed at the water's edge by the uneasy call of the Great Northern Diver.

These woods on whose borders in winter the caribou browse the lichen under the snow; these swift rivers where the salmon leap; these plateaus here and there denuded of forest, and the peaty soil of which grows fabulous plants. The *sarracenia purpurea* or "Wildman's cup" whose red veined leaves are also a vase in which, on hot days, the rare traveller finds refreshing water; the Indian Pipe whose stem, leaves, and flower seem carved from a piece of ivory: the Fly Catcher whose little leaves, rough with red viscous spikes hold prisoner the imprudent insect who came there to seek a place in the sun; and many others that could be plucked without stopping the carriage.

The first stop is at the half-way house, a little cottage from which one sees a mournful group of mountains lifelessly stretched under a dark shroud of firs. Then, at Carys, is another inn where we make our final halt. There is one in the middle of a farm near a torrent. There is life, noise, and in the already profound darkness the coming and going of lighted lanterns on carriages that are bringing or taking the caribou-hunters or salmon fishermen. This place is famous among sportsmen.

Then the rest of the trip—an hour's drive in heavy shadows on a narrow road that no parapet protects from the precipice that drops from its side down to the sea in Salmonier. Our songs sent French echoes sounding through these solitudes where ordinarily the only voice that murmurs is that of the sea breeze which comes in the evening to wake the sounds of the forest. And our irruption at midnight at the home of Father St. John, where a good supper made us forget all poetry in thinking of nothing but satisfying our greedy appetites. Then the two rooms reserved for the French Consul and myself in the finest house in the village, and the rest of the night passed without sleep, thanks to the inhospitable bawling of an infant.

Next day the sun was one of the party. First we got in a boat and, leaving the sea, we entered a river bordered in the most picturesque fashion by high rocks covered with lush vegetation. At every bend there were surprises and changes of scenery of the most remarkable variety. At lunchtime we crossed the arm to the other side where Father St. John is building a church that is almost finished. We went in and set up a table with some planks and spread our provisions on it. It is thus that the church was inaugurated while waiting for its consecration; but among the revelers were three priests all ready to give us absolution. Here we are with a new pretext for observations on manners and I wish to note some others as well before I arrive at the moment—a moment long desired—when I can write "Finis" to the last page of my journal.

FATHER JOHN ST. JOHN. "I know of no clergy more tolerant or more respected, taking so great a part in the contacts of everyday life and enjoying so great a reputation for sanctity."

First it should be mentioned that it is Father Galveston, brother-in-law of Father St. John, who, in concert with him, had organized our excursion. The feminine element, far from being lacking, was represented in the most charming manner. For three days in the carriage, in the boat, on foot, at table, everybody came together or dispersed with the most complete liberty of movement. You find this extraordinary. Doubtless you have reasons for that, but out here no one sees any harm. I know of no clergy more tolerant or more respected, taking so great a part in the contacts of everyday life and enjoying so great a reputation for sanctity. I need say no more about that. I have spoken enough about it elsewhere. But I found most intriguing this detail of completely temporal pleasure shared without hesitation or surprise between the priest and his flock.

But it's not a fixed idea of mine to approve everything in the customs of Anglo-Americans. Far from it. I was even very much shocked by an incident which took place one evening at a ball at the home of a charming young woman. All of a sudden there was a row on the stairs. I went to see; it was the commander of an English cruiser who, on the pretext that his servant had a dispute with another, was fighting with the latter.

September 7th—I was most astonished this morning to receive a letter from Miss Esther, a note expressed thus: "Would you be so kind as to escort us, my sister and myself, on board the *Tenedos*. My father and brother have to be absent." It was a dance which was to be held on board the flagship of the English Squadron. I hastened to accept, proud of my role, and some hours afterwards we embarked and mounted the deck of the *Tenedos*. I let my two

SALMONIER CHURCH. "At lunch time we crossed the arm to the other side where Father St. John is building a church that is almost finished."

young ladies each go her own way and, noting Miss Lilia, I sat down with her to chat in the embrasure of a porthole. She also had come alone with friends whose parents had stayed at home.

I like flirting with Lilia. I found her of a singular charm. It was neither love nor friendship but something more tender than friendship and less indiscreet than love. Flirting! Who has ever said what it is? Where does it commence and where does it finish? Everyone tends to believe that it lies halfway between gallantry on one side and love on the other; but where is the exact line of demarcation? We Frenchmen are ignorant of this sentiment. Let us not doubt that it will produce sensations both profound and delicate.

Is it not charming to penetrate, little by little, the heart of a young girl and end by making oneself a place there without falling into the indifference of a too easy comradeship or into the too strict bonds of a love affair? But the saying of the Great King remains true always and in all places. Today, what is truth on one side of the ocean is a lie on the other. This intimate commerce between the sexes—perfectly honourable here—would be doubtless very dangerous in France. I think custom has very little to do with this but only character. There are here two young people who soon will no longer be so, who are engaged for 10 years and for 10 years have remained so. A thousand impediments have prevented their marriage. They waited until all obstacles had been cleared away and then they were married. Almost always they are engaged for a year or two. Many for three or four years.

Speak of that to a Frenchman. You will see that to him it is to ask the impossible. And it is the same for flirting. Indeed, the character of the two people is so different that the bringing-up of French girls is no less a subject of consternation for the Americans than that of Americans for the French. In revenge, I believe that married women are the same in every country.

The other day, Lady S— gave a party in honour of Prince George, the second son of the Prince of Wales, a midshipman on the cruiser *Canada*.[34] Her pride as mistress of the house turned her head and the day before, as French taste is a law everywhere, she came to consult us on the decoration of her rooms. The evening was most animated. Prince George, with whom I had the honour of speaking French, never missed a dance. His ship left next day and Lady S— could not conceal her triumph at being the only one who could flatter herself that she had received His Royal Highness.

September 20th—This morning I was present at a ceremony which is doubtless the last that I shall honour with my presence. It was at the Presentation Convent which had invited us to a celebration for its 50th anniversary. There was first a Pontifical Mass in the chapel. During this, they most disgracefully skinned alive the Mass of Saint Cecelia and, not content with this first crime, they went on to profane the "Inflammatus" of the "Stabat

MOTHER MARY MAGDALEN O'SHAUGHNESSY. *"The Superior of the Convent, one of the four sisters who came here fifty years ago, was there bent over a prie-dieu."*

Mater." After the ceremony Father Galveston gave a short history of the foundation of women's convents in Newfoundland. Fifty years ago, he told us, the four sisters who came to found this convent were the first religious of English speech who had yet crossed the ocean. Goodbyes were said to them as to people who were leaving for a country situated in another world from which they would never return. When they disembarked at St. John's the doctor's carriage was put at their disposal as it was the only one on the Island. The Superior of the Convent, one of the four sisters who came here 50 years ago, was there bent over a prie-dieu.[35] The ceremony finished with a hymn where at last they did us the grace to give us an "0 Salutaris" by Miss Fisher composed by Cherubini.[36]

A luncheon was waiting for us in a large room. The Bishop, with his usual gaiety, presided over the vast horseshoe table around which were seated a number of young ladies and the clergy of the Cathedral. Toasts were drunk at the dessert. All this was in the Convent, in the reception room of which we were treated to a concert after we had left the table.

October 3rd—We brought home from hunting several snipe and half a dozen partridges. About ten miles from St. John's, we stopped the carriage and started to hunt over ground that was totally unfamiliar. Then, led on by our war-like enthusiasm, we pushed on over the swamps and hills without paying attention, so that once *en route* we did not know whether we should turn right or left. Naturally we went in the wrong direction; we walked for a long time and could not find either the carriage or a familiar locality when we saw the sea between two hills.

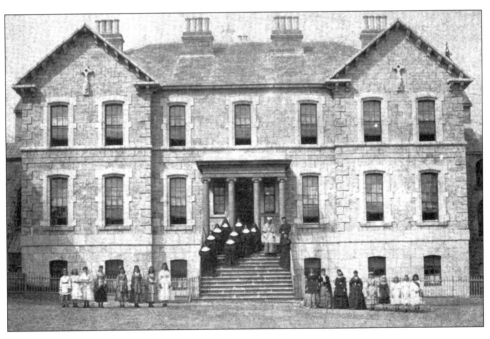

PRESENTATION CONVENT. "A luncheon was waiting for us in a large room. The Bishop, with his usual gaiety, presided over the vast horseshoe table around which were seated a number of young ladies and the clergy of the Cathedral."

As we had not seen it on the way in, it was clear that we were on the wrong path. We went back on our tracks always without seeing any familiar territory. Some women passed us and I questioned them, but they had not seen our carriage and could give us no direction.

Night was coming on. One of us remarked that the moon was turning up the wick of her lamp. We fired a volley from our guns and hurled strident shouts into the echoes. Then we listened, but there was no answer. Nothing but the pale and dusty line of the road that disappeared a short distance away behind a grey rock and little stunted bushes, low and tufted, where the passing dusk left streaks of its cold and somber veil: silence, always the great silence of the wilderness. It slept, lazily spread over its lakes or perched like a solitary lizard on the mass, eternally immobile, of the naked rocks. Only from time to time there was the cry of a frightened bird. The west wind raised ripples on all this sleeping nature and we could hear the regular sound of our hurried steps.

Suddenly, a distant heavy sound—increasing always, then discordant and noisy— came to disturb this dreaming calm. It's our carriage. That's it. It's really it. We had simply gone a lot farther than the place agreed for our meeting and, becoming anxious at not seeing us, the driver had come to meet us. He had not wasted his journey since, in passing by the lakes and streams, he had caught 114 trout. That's the way it is in Newfoundland. An hour before dinner one can go to the nearest stream and bring back a dozen trout and toss them still alive into the frying pan.

October 20th—Everything passes and everything comes to pass, even what one is wishing for. At the bottom of this page I should write the word FINIS, always a cruel word since it means happiness forever ended or misery endured to the end. And thus it is that, in spite of my ardent desire to go back to France, I am aware that I cannot, without regrets, leave forever a country where I have passed so many hours of youth. Sad or gay hardly matters, some part of me will stay here for ever. I hardly dare to finish this page and my pen, in spite of me, traces these verses in place of the fatal word.[37]

Oh my country, my memories
That I invoked in this naked land,
I thought that all my sighs
Just to the last would be for you. Illusion!
The hour of departure sounds
And the joy of seeing you again, my France,
Doesn't prevent a single look
From leaving a touch of bitter sadness.
My poor heart, all astonished
To feel that in this land,
Something of itself was given.

PART III

A FUGUE IN NORTH AMERICA

We were now in the Narrows. On one side was the lighthouse and on the other the old remains of the French fortifications. Here and there, in the clefts of the rocks, were the little homes of the fishermen with their flakes for drying cod.

1

St. John's to Halifax

W E WERE two days waiting at St. John's for the *Nova Scotia*, the best steamer of the Allan Line, which runs the service between Liverpool and Baltimore. She came at last, after having escaped the assaults of a sea already running high from equinoctial winds. The next day was the 20th of October and it was on this day, on a fine morning, I left the Colony, the most ancient of the English possessions in North America and where I had passed 17 months as temporary attaché to the Vice-Consulate of France. At last they fired the gun, signal for our sailing, and half an hour after, we dropped the mooring that held us to the wharf; then the screw threshed the water and we slowly crept into the stream. From the shore, they could see as we turned how the huge vessel seemed to shorten as the bow and stern came into line and the three masts seemed to be as one. How often has this spectacle been for me the best amusement of the week.

Grouped on the deck, we watched the harbour which seemed to be going away from us while the hills on the other side seemed to be coming to meet us. On the shore, faces could no longer be identified, but the fluttering hand-kerchiefs prolonged the farewells. Finally, we could only see them as a cloud of white butterflies flickering in an occasional beam of light. Stacked one above another on the hills, the houses of the town mingled their slate roofs and crowded more and more upon each other. When the wind spread it, one could still see the colours of the flag which fluttered from the staff of the French Consulate. I sent a farewell in its direction and then I could see nothing more except the Catholic cathedral, whose rearing towers gave the effect of mounting closer and closer to the sky.

We were now in the Narrows. On one side was the lighthouse and on the other the old remains of the French fortifications. Here and there, in the clefts of the rocks, were the little homes of the fishermen with their flakes for drying cod. At this point, it's only about 400 yards wide and when it is passed, the cliffs seem to close up behind. Soon they are no longer separated except by a narrow cleft through which one can still see the last buildings of St. John's. Then the two walls suddenly join, and one has before one's eyes only an indented coast without any sign of a harbour and, advancing on all sides, its armoured strength as if to defend itself from attacking weapons.

I now left my observation post. It was over at last. St. John's had disappeared forever. It seemed to me swallowed up with all its inhabitants in the arms of the hills which had suddenly snatched it out of sight. A vague sadness came over me and I looked about me to see if I could find a companion with whom I could talk over a past so quickly vanished. Heaven sent me one. Arriving on the Halifax packet, he had barely touched at St. John's, where I happened to meet him at the home of a charming girl.

This mutual acquaintance served as an excuse for our reunion, and as one forms ties as easily on the bridge of a ship as in a private room, we set ourselves to walking side by side and taking stock of each other as might two gallant knights of olden times who met on the road to Jerusalem. This comparison is not as far-fetched as might appear, for what did we speak of if it was not the "fair damsels" that we had left behind us and of the country towards which the prow of our ship was pointed?

We had two days and nights to pass on board before landing at Halifax. It's true that the trip promised to be fine. The sea, doubtless tired of being so angry for the preceding days, fell into an almost flat calm. The wind, which nonetheless still kept up, raised only little waves which lazily rolled their foaming crests one over the other and, happy to see this same ocean, so fierce yesterday, now fawning at her feet, our vessel resolutely sailed straight on.

There was no fog and we traversed the coast at a few cables' length. From time to time, we could see little settlements crouching at the end of a bay among the firs and birches, or we crossed some fishing boat with swelling sails which fled erratically through our wake. They went almost as fast as we did, in the opposite direction, and disappeared quickly below the horizon. By evening they would be in St. John's and would bring our thoughts there again for a moment. In spite of all that, time is long at sea when one has no close friend with one. One tires quickly of the company of people one scarcely knows, so after lunch, where we found each other at the Captain's table, my "friend" and I kept to ourselves.

I had then taken up again my solitary walk on deck when I was greeted by a young man with refined and regular features and big brown eyes that lit up an intelligent face. He spoke my name. I stopped in surprise and looked at him and he explained that, having seen my name on the passenger list, he said to himself that I must be its owner as I didn't look like an Englishman. Delighted to find somebody to talk to in my own language, I matched my pace with his, and thanks to his company the rest of the day did not seem so long. This unfortunate chap didn't speak a word of English and nobody on board understood French. He was Polish and had suffered a host of misfortunes, following which he was filled with a violent hatred of the English. He had embarked two months before on a steamer going to New York. They had nearly foundered in mid-ocean, when happily a steamer had come to their rescue and towed them to St. John's. But what made him furious was that, once there, the passengers had presented an address of thanks to the Captain who had exposed them to the danger of shipwreck.

At last on the morning of the third day, just 44 hours after leaving St. John's, we arrived at Halifax, the Capital of Nova Scotia, at the end of a beautiful trip. From now on we were on the American continent and in the Dominion of Canada. Newfoundland is not part of this Confederation. It is an absolutely independent colony which governs itself and whose supreme head, the Queen's representative, has scarcely any more power than has the Queen herself in England. On the contrary, there is only a Lieutenant-Governor in Halifax and he is responsible to the Governor General in Ottawa.

But let us not go faster than our steamer, which is still only at the entrance to the roadstead, and let us commence by studying the outer aspect of the country before seeking to know its organization. The coast is very different from Newfoundland. In place of cliffs, there are here flat lands gently rising to enclose the bay with their wooded undulations. They offer no shelter from the winds and the vast space they enclose can offer no anchorage to a ship. At the end of half an hour we passed, to starboard, a little fortified island whose green carpet threw a note of gaiety in the middle of the sky-grey sea. On the heights to the left rises the Citadel. The semaphore lifts and signals us to the fort with its long arms. We reply with two successive shots and commence to go past the town, which is on the port side. We pass it almost completely in review and its buildings, that show themselves in turn, make a good impression.

Finally we docked and our baggage was soon landed. It went directly from the wharf to the Customs opposite. A valise and two bags were enough to excite the suspicion of the official, who asked if I had a lady with me. On my replying in the negative, he made me open one of my boxes, but was satisfied with my lifting the cover.

An old carriage harnessed with two white horses soon dropped me at the Halifax Hotel. It's a fine big establishment that was recommended to me and that I also recommend to those of my readers who will have the whim to make a tour of Nova Scotia. By good luck I knew a charming family in this town— a doctor and his wife, the latter from one of the best and most agreeable families in St. John's. I went to see them between breakfast and lunch and, as it was Sunday and Mass-time, I went with them to the Catholic cathedral. It was a fine building in the Gothic style, but alas, I can't say the same for the music I heard there.

After Mass they very graciously kept me for lunch and I ate, for the first time, those American partridges that roost in the fir trees and whose succulent flesh is as white as a pheasant's. The town that I perambulated afterwards seemed a great city compared with St. John's—paved streets with real sidewalks aligned between fine houses and public buildings of cut stone, avenues planted with fine old trees and lined with splendid mansions. Besides, on that day I couldn't judge everything, as the shops were closed and the people had stayed at home to keep the Sabbath day holy. I therefore decided to pass the time by writing and to wait until the morrow to explore the city.

I made my first visit to the railway station. It's a building that on the outside resembles a palace, but the inside is only a big shed where everyone comes freely. Baggage registration is easy and cheap. They attach a number to your bag and give you a duplicate, just as in the cloak room of our theatres, and all it costs you is the trouble of carrying with you as many numbers as you have bags. On leaving the station I saw the English Squadron in port. There was the *Northampton* flying the flag of the Admiral, Sir J.E. Commerell, V.A., K.C.B.[38] Her heavy armoured flanks seemed as if built on undersea foundations. I had seen her in Newfoundland a few weeks before, as well as the other

vessels of the Squadron including the *Canada*, of which Prince George, the son of the Prince of Wales, was a midshipman. At St. John's, they had given a ball for him at which I had the honour to be presented and where I chatted with him in French.

I crossed the Public Gardens and climbed the fortifications as far as the base of the semaphore. Dominating the whole scene from there, I saw one of the most beautiful panoramas one can imagine. One's view is lost on one side in the changing distance of the sea. Two islands, the more distant of which is large and wooded, swim in the middle of the roadstead. The other is a little fort which commands the entrance to the port. In front of me were hills, gently undulating and covered with fine vegetation. Folded in the nook of a valley and wetting its feet in the ocean was a suburb of the town with its white steeple.

To the left, the sea forms a waterway forcing its way through the land, disappearing and re-appearing in turn through the trees right to the horizon. At my feet,

ADMIRAL JOHN EDWARD COMMERELL. "On leaving the station I saw the English Squadron in port. There was the *Northampton*, flying the flag of the Admiral."

on the bank where I am placed, the town extends. The activity of a great city spreads continually over a line of many miles of wide streets. I remained a long while watching this spectacle, as imposing as it was varied, and on my way back I met some English soldiers in red jackets and white helmets.

I returned towards the lower town where the Halifax Hotel was situated and wondered whether this evening I would start for New York or Canada, when I met an English ship captain whom I knew. He asked me to come and see him but I told him I was leaving in a few hours for Quebec, and this decided me. I went in, strapped my bags, and went to get my ticket for the ancient capital of Canada.

These agencies, where one can get one's ticket without need to go to the station half an hour before train time, are a great convenience in America. One can even get them the day before. They will give you one valid for a certain number of days or even for an indefinite period and for the whole length of the line. Thus, mine would bring me to Montreal, with licence to spend ten days on the journey.

The sun, all red and enormous, rose on a flat and empty country whose forests of fir and birch, as far as the eye could reach, were covered with a thick coat of hoar-frost, although it was only the 24th of October.

2

HALIFAX TO QUEBEC, MONTREAL AND CAUGHNAWAGA

OUR sleeping car was full leaving Halifax, but I didn't know any of my travelling companions. After a good enough night in a bed where a bigger man than I could have stretched out at his ease, the cold woke me at daylight. As we were not due to arrive until ten o'clock at night, I was in no hurry to dress. I put up my window blinds and, since on the other side a curtain protected me from indirect observation, I watched, half leaning on my cot, the countryside that unrolled alongside the train.

The sun, all red and enormous, rose on a flat and empty country whose forests of fir and birch, as far as the eye could reach, were covered with a thick coat of hoar-frost, although it was only the 24th of October. About seven o'clock we saw a village picturesquely scattered around a large bay; the smooth sea reflected the pale rays of the early light; the earth, the streams and the marshes shivered beneath their mantle of ice.

However, the countryside took on another character. The eternal scrub firs mingled with little birches became rarer—suddenly, here was the sea again. It will soon be eight o'clock. The corridor that divides our car lengthways begins to fill with the movements of those who are getting up and are going to shave and dress their hair in the bathroom. I lift my curtain a little and, behind those of my neighbours, I see their limbs showing and hands held out to lace shoes and the curtain-material that bulges and falls back at each movement of the person in putting on a shirt or lacing a corset. When I am sufficiently initiated into the manner of behaving in an American sleeping car, I lean back on my elbow and return to my magic lantern.

The immense tablecloth of silent and motionless water, white on the bank where we pass, is mingled with all the shades of blue when it dies out at a horizon bounded by roughly silhouetted mountains, less blue than the waters bathing them and less pale than the encompassing sky. They run towards the north, drowning their last peaks far away where the sea and sky meet and mix. There, they resemble only a light mist already vanishing. On the other hand, they lift up again to the south, swathed in more sombre colours. From the immense amphitheatre, there protrude many wooded islands which can be clearly distinguished from the gauzy background of morning light.

The foreground, that is to say the bank we are traversing, is gay with little rustic houses spreading their poor roofs in the shadow of the copses with their multicoloured trees and gives the finishing touch to this picture. I don't know the Gulf of Naples, but certainly this place that they call Baie Chaleur makes one dream of everything that the imagination can call up of the abundant and poetic, and such a place, in Europe, would make the fortune of anyone who found it.

From there on we never ceased to run through a most varied countryside, the railway running perpetually along the torrents closed in between hills that were covered with firs and birch. I could see from the gangway where I stood, the salmon sleeping in the swift and shallow waters, while on the borders of the road long needles of ice hung from the rocks. There were green trees of many kinds, spruce, larch, etc., white birch, spindle trees with purple boughs, the rowan with its red berries and, on the ground, a little plant that created a red carpet. All this spread over hills, plateaus, ravines, convolutions, surveys, and crossed by the railway. This is the general aspect of the country as far as Rimouski. The autumn colours have a variety and brilliance peculiar to North America and this is the season favoured by tourists for travelling.

At Rimouski one hears nothing but French spoken on the station platform and one sees the spread of the St. Lawrence, more like a gulf than a river. From one side to the other is so far that we would take it for the sea if the high mountains did not lift their pale-grey tips in the blue distance. It was more than 30 hours since we had left Halifax when finally the train left us at Point Levis. Point Levis is a suburb of Quebec situated on the left bank of the St. Lawrence. One must cross the river on a ferryboat which lands you at the town wharf. These ferryboats are a sort of floating house run by steam on which one embarks on foot or by carriage and there are many of them on the large American rivers, wherever a bridge might interfere with navigation.

It had been night for a long time and one could see only the lights of Quebec which, here and there, starred the water of the river with trembling flickers of light. Being unable to see the countryside, I chatted with a young man that I had known for some hours.

I noticed gradually on the trip that the greater part of the passengers were French-Canadians, and several started conversations with me. One of them told me he intended passing the following day at Quebec, and would leave in the evening for Montreal.

He was free from all engagements and proposed to me that I stay at the same hotel as himself and, afterwards, that we make the journey to Montreal together. At Quebec, he would serve as my guide. This project suited my plans and I accepted.

I had been told that the Hotel St. Louis was the best. I spoke to him of it, but he was used to another one and brought me with him. It was a sort of inn, as I could tell right away by its appearance and the plebian manners of some men collected in the common room.

I made up my mind quickly, feeling that it was not improper for a traveller to seek an occasional adventure. I was named and introduced and I must say from there on was treated with particular regard. Never mind that I had to go into a double room, and what a room! And what beds! And what washbasins! And then, next morning, as I was taking some notes in my journal on my pillow, while my companion still snored, I was suddenly interrupted by his acquaintances, who entered like a storm to say good morning to their friend. Being no longer able to write because of their prattle, I got up. I was introduced, they called for madeira, and they drank my health.

After breakfast we went out. Quebec, being built on a sort of cliff in the middle of the river, looks from far off very picturesque. When one is there, one is only conscious of the trouble of climbing up and down again. The town is neither beautiful nor interesting. I expected to find interesting old houses: but all stamp of antiquity has disappeared under modern paint. However, there is something magnificent, or at least imposing, in the vast terrace which stretches at the foot of the Citadel where the St. Lawrence presents a panorama that might count, without exaggeration, as one of the most beautiful in the world.

In the afternoon, the manager of the hotel, a pleasant young fellow, took me to the Citadel. There, one of his friends, a cavalry sergeant, well turned out and well-informed, guided us with a friendliness and warmth altogether Canadian, which is saying a lot. He spoke French with correctness and much more distinctly than most French-Canadians whom I have met and whose speech is often impossible to understand. If I had not resolved to name nobody here I would be happy to write his name and to thank him again for the manner in which he did the honours of the Citadel...including an excellent glass of beer.

From the ramparts, one sees on all sides a series of panoramas that are like the dreams of a scene painter for the opera. What one should look for in Quebec are these dominating lookouts. In the Citadel are only infantry and artillery, but there was some question of adding light cavalry, and it was with this in view that they had seconded the young subaltern who accompanied us.

A fairly strong garrison is not useless at Quebec. The lower town, partly occupied by poor houses between which wind dirty and narrow streets, is populated by Irishmen on whose part one may always fear some political manifestation. Two or three years before my arrival, the Marquis of Lansdowne being come to Canada to replace Governor General the Marquis of Lorne, a relative of the queen, arrived at Quebec. The Irish did not like him, although his predecessor had known how to engage their sympathies, as he did those of everyone. They agitated and protested against his nomination, although a peaceful settlement was achieved.

The Governor General is housed in the very stronghold of the Citadel when he comes to Quebec. One must not believe, as many people do, that the ancient capital of *Canada* has remained that of the *Dominion*. It is at Ottawa, a town in the north on a tributary of the St. Lawrence, and already having 40,000 people, although it is of very recent origin, that Great Britain has established the seat of government of her American provinces. From there the Governor General extends his authority over all the other English colonies of this region, excepting Newfoundland, which as I have said, is independent of all other authority except the Queen's.

However, every province of Canada has its own capital, with its own Parliament which deals with all matters pertaining especially to the province. Quebec is one of these capitals, and they have built a noble edifice in which the Houses sit. As far as other monuments are concerned, there is nothing very remarkable in the city, which is nonetheless the most ancient in Canada. It was founded by Champlain in 1608. Wolfe took it in 1759 after the glorious defeat in which Montcalm perished. From the Citadel, they show you the battlefield of the Plains of Abraham where there rears a monument in honour of the two heroes. One can visit the University, a vast building which houses the many halls of a museum of painting, natural history etc., and above all a splendid library of 70,000 volumes.

All this is in the upper town. The lower town is entirely commercial. Before going down, let us not forget to see everything. It's not worth the trouble to bring the reader to the Cathedral. I would rather ask him to accompany me to the market square to a great manufacturer of pianos and organs. My companion, who knows him, introduced me to him, and since he knows I am a musician, he opens and makes me try one after another of his instruments. However, he failed to convince me that the manufacturers of overseas are as skillful as are ours. No matter how excellent are Weber's pianos, which are the style in America at the moment, I still give the palm to those of Erard, Pleyel, etc.

Thinking perhaps that I would appreciate his eloquence more, this good fellow took us to the bar of the Hotel St. Louis. All the while he kept up an endless political discussion which would certainly have interested me if I could have understood it. I had need to stretch my curious traveller's ears but it was impossible to get a word of this gibberish-French. Besides, the Canadian "you know" that he placed regularly between each word succeeded in derailing me completely. This personage is certainly the most extraordinary thing I met in Quebec. For all that, he was pleasant and shrewd, like all his compatriots, and could, if I had been able to understand him, have furnished me numerous details of great interest. He was well read in the history of his country and was a member of the municipal council.

As for my roommate, I saw with annoyance that it was useless to ask him any question, incapable as he was of responding. My last glance, before regaining my inn, was for the harbour. There is considerable work being done to enlarge it and the workmen pursue their task at night by electric light.

One day sufficed me to see Quebec and my readers will know this hospitable town as well as I do when I add that it is the seat of our Consulate General for North America and that the great Allan Liners, which ply between Liverpool and Montreal, come and go there every eight days. In the evening I embarked for Montreal on one of those river steamers whose two funnels always gave such a picturesque effect in pictures of "An American River."

Next morning, after 12 hours of travel, we landed at Montreal, and this time, in place of following my companion, I stuck to the instructions I had been given and had myself brought to the Windsor Hotel. It is a sort of palace, situated outside the town and established on the American Plan. There are, in America, two different kinds of hotel: those on the American Plan, where for a sum varying from three to five dollars, one is lodged, fed and served: and those on the European Plan where one pays for everything separately and according as one uses it.

I had scarcely arrived and was going out to see the town when I met the German Trade Agent from Newfoundland.[39] He was astonished to see me, and making himself my guide, he introduced me to all his friends, saying that I had appeared to him like the Angel Gabriel. His society made my stay at Montreal all the more agreeable, for he offered me a place at his table between two young and lovely widows that he was conducting on a business trip. We went out after breakfast. Beautiful shops, beautiful streets, beautiful monuments and crowds of well-dressed women, all these things that I had not seen for so long gave me a most agreeable surprise.

Montreal is the biggest and most important town in Canada and may well become the most populous and active center in North America. It is situated on an island in the St. Lawrence at the mouth of the Ottawa River and has a population of about 300,000 souls.

Its prodigious increase has made it a redoubtable neighbour for Chicago and it's not difficult to foresee that, with the finishing of the Canadian Pacific Railway, Montreal will eclipse its rival. The first European came there in the middle of the 16th century. There was there, then, an Indian village called "Hochelaga." The majority of the inhabitants are Catholic and French. However, outside of the common people and the shopkeepers, English is spoken as much as French. From the very first day I was brought by the German Consul to meet many traders and I was very quickly able to convince myself of the important business done at Montreal. The largest steamers come up the St. Lawrence to there and moor along the quays, which are superb.

If one reflects that Montreal is more than 800 kilometres from the sea, and that for another 200 towards Lake Ontario the St. Lawrence maintains a width of at least a kilometre, one can get an idea of the immensity of this river. As for the island of Montreal, it's about 30 kilometres long and 15 wide. The right bank is connected with the town by an iron bridge more than three kilometres long.

Near the Windsor Hotel is Mount Royal. It's a beautiful park, planted with large-leaved oaks, which climbs a high hill from which one sees a superb view of the town and the river. There are long streets with a succession of elegant mansions

ROBERT HENRY PROWSE. "His society made my stay at Montreal all the more agreeable, for he offered me a place at his table between two young and lovely widows that he was conducting on a business trip."

with forecourts and gardens stretching far out to the western extremity of the island: in front, one sees the right branch of the St. Lawrence with its harbour full of shipping, but one cannot see the left branch and so one has no impression of being on an island.

I had known some young men from Montreal in Newfoundland. On the evening of my arrival, I was invited to the home of one of them. The family was one of the most important in the place and lived in one of these lovely mansions I have spoken of. After a very good dinner we went to the theatre, where they presented a drama followed by a comedy. What pleasure it was to find myself in a real theatre again after 18 months in the darkness, far from the footlights. I suddenly decided to prolong my stay in this friendly city and the following day I decided, with two other young men, to make an excursion to an Indian village situated on the St. Lawrence about 16 miles above Montreal.

We left in the daytime, and at the end of half an hour the train put us down on the left bank of the St. Lawrence. There we got into an Indian canoe that brought us to the opposite bank. In this place the river is very wide and scattered with islands covered with high copses. We had two miles to go before we landed on the nearest point on the other side, but our light craft propelled by short paddles glided rapidly through the water, and we soon landed at the purely Indian village of Caughnawaga.⁴⁰

Doubtless you may expect to find in the following lines descriptions of huts, feathered headdresses and poisoned arrows. I prefer to destroy the reader's illusions at once for fear that he might accuse me afterwards of artfully trying to capture his interest. There are, at Caughnawaga, only wooden houses such as one sees everywhere in Canada. They are aligned without order on both sides of a single street, distinguished from the surrounding terrain by more and deeper ruts. If one wishes to flounder even more, one has only to cross the little square in front of the church. This lifts its single spire next to the priest's house, for all are Catholics at Caughnawaga. Everyone also is Iroquois, for no white man has the right to settle there by fiat of the Canadian Government. Thanks to this circumstance, one finds here the true type of Indian, in all its purity.

They are fine men with broad shoulders, aquiline noses, shining teeth, a dark and profound eye with a glance that is sometimes brilliant and sometimes melancholy. Those who stick to the remains of the old traditions have long hair, dark and glossy, falling to their shoulders. The women have complexions less dark than the men and I have seen some that were almost white and very pretty.

After dinner we went to the house of the head chief who, alas, has the English name of William. I should say that one of the young men I was with has a house there where he spends several days a week because of certain functions he exercises for the Government. He is respected and consulted by everybody and he received us there like a prince in the middle of his vassals. He explained to me that the village is governed by a head chief and four minor chiefs, but that in all matters of law the Indians are regarded as children and

CAUGHNAWAGA, QUEBEC. "There are, at Caughnawaga, only wooden houses such as one sees everywhere in Canada. They are aligned without order on both sides of a single street, distinguished from the surrounding terrain by more and deeper ruts."

minors and placed under the tutelage of the Dominion Government. As soon as she saw us, the wife of the head chief hastened to make us come in.

In spite of his great dignity, Williams kept a shop for groceries and other merchandise. One goes in by the shop and then to two big rooms, of which the first is a dining room and the other a reception room. In one I saw, with admiration, a sort of monument, with rampant lions, made of beads of all colours. The Indians excel in this kind of work and I had before my eyes a veritable masterpiece, for it had taken the first prize in an exhibition that my friend had organized in the village.

But in the other rooms—oh horrid sight, against the wall at the back. Alas no, not scalps or other spoils of Christians but a piano: and to make it worse a grand piano displays its ugly belly, wallowing in civilization. Fortunately the chief's wife speaks only Iroquois and I console myself by looking at her.

However, our presence being announced, the company hasten to see us. First of all was the daughter of the Head Chief. She is 14 years old but is already self-possessed, and very grave, a real young lady (It's desolating, but I can find no other suitable word). She speaks English better than I do and French almost as well. Several men enter. All speak those two terrible languages. Finally, the young lady sits down at the piano and plays some waltzes that I recognize from hearing them at two Parisian salons.

I sulked completely when they asked me, in turn, to play some music but I satisfied them and as they covered me with exaggerated compliments, I profited by asking them for some Iroquois songs.

They knew a number of these and some sang in chorus and some sang solo. I vamped an accompaniment, striving to draw the most savage chords from the instrument…and I succeeded. I closed my eyes, trying to forget all civilization, and listened with delight to the Indian melody flowing along on soft and harmonious words like the whisper of a breeze in the vines. Some of them had fine voices and they are all generally musicians. The chief's daughter did herself credit on the piano. They badly wanted me to sing, and as they had sung their national songs for me I tried to think of one from my country and intoned "Au Clair de la Lune" which they applauded loudly. The Head Chief's wife cried "Sago" which means "Encore" and I had to do it over again, just like mademoiselle Van Zant in the romance of Lakmé.

Before we left, Williams showed us some very curious antiques, but he kept them as relics of his ancestors and I couldn't get anything to take away. However, I didn't leave altogether as I came, for I had learned several Iroquois words. These, for example, which will give a faint idea of the language: "aona" good-bye..."sego" which means both "good day" and "encore" "ouxsa" meaning "do it quickly" or "hurry up" and "conoronghquoa" meaning "my dear."

We were up next morning at four o'clock. Having fed like Englishmen, we put our guns on our shoulders and left the sleeping village of Caughnawaga. In the calm night, the mist that silvered the light of the stars, rendered the surrounding objects rather confused. Suddenly my two companions stopped. I noticed something dark, which barred our passage. One of them bent down and I saw that he was pushing something that seemed to glide. It was an Indian canoe. All three of us got in, making it rock terribly on the dark water. Then, with silent paddles, we set ourselves to push through the thick clumps of reeds and rushes.

Soon we could hear the flutter of wings, low cackling, the splash of a dive. We directed ourselves by these, butting sometimes against invisible obstacles, then we would stop, ears cocked. Then the ducks, for it was these we hunted, would be heard on another side and made us keep shuttling back and forth on the sleepy St. Lawrence.

Finally dawn began to break. According as the light increased, the river grew more vast around us. The dawn spread grey light that gave a hazy reflection to each object. Then we commenced firing, sometimes at a bit of floating wood, sometimes at leaves or patches of greenery floating in the stream and which we took for web-footed creatures. However, after one burst of fire, the object seen had disappeared. It soon showed nearer us and swimming towards us. Three successive blasts and the lead that ricocheted about him did not stop him in his courageous march against the enemy. I heard one of my companions say "It's a muskrat." This name also evoked in my mind a thousand exciting pictures of "The Trappers of the Arkansas." I put the weapon to my shoulder as if I had before me a whole tribe of Comanche or Crow Indians and I pulled both triggers one after the other.

When the cloud of smoke thinned out, we saw the heroic animal appear ready to climb into our canoe; but it only advanced with the speed of the current. It was killed, and seizing it by its knife blade tail, my companion reached it towards me so that I could smell the odour of musk.

Daylight suddenly came completely as if, uncertain at first, it had at last suddenly decided to appear. Then we made long tacks on the river but always staying on the same side. Around ten o'clock, tired by this work, we returned to breakfast. Two hours after, we returned, but in another direction and this time with a long-haired Iroquois to direct our canoe. The whole thing was very picturesque. We didn't leave the river until evening, but neither guile nor patience helped us to our purpose of getting near the numerous flocks of ducks. Towards the end of the day, despairing of all success, we took to firing unlikely shots for the simple fun of it.

We landed on different islands covered with tufts of vegetation, where my companions noted several birds that were unknown to me. Finally the invading night chased us from the river, and I believe that if they had served me my muskrat for dinner, I would have found it good. In spite of our unsuccessful hunt, I congratulated myself sincerely on our day. What is so admirable as this river, the largest in America and which in many places has only the sky for horizon.

I had, besides, been particularly favoured. The day of our hunt was under a pale-blue sky, the St. Lawrence spread before us a cloth of white barred with flecks of blue. From the Great Lakes whence it comes in all its majesty, one sees it flow, dividing its waters around numerous islands; the further ones showing only the whitish tops of their trees fading against the sky. The ones nearer to us, and forming the foreground, gave vivid contrasts by reason of their autumn foliage. At the right, on the far shore, one could see two convents of nuns, tranquil amongst their high trees. On the left the Indian village scattered its little houses on the bare bank like a fisherman's net drying on the green.

There was limpidity in the air and the water that would make one dizzy; there were clear distances that the eye could not capture, diaphanous depths all filled with air, shadows full of warm and vivid colour; there was something varied and splendid about everything; and at evening, as the sun sank, a blue shadow extinguished one by one each ray of light.

Sometimes the great silence was troubled by a low drumming, whose vibrations trembled on the water around us. All of a sudden, one saw appearing far away, the two black funnels of a steamer. She showed up against the sky and soon the ship herself surged over the river with her two great wheels which sent the flocks of duck flying. She stopped at a landing place on the shore opposite Caughnawaga and awaited passengers from the train, who preferred to go down by boat as far as Montreal. It was at this place we were to take her the following morning to run the dangerous Lachine rapids.

Today, when we leave the hospitable roofs of the Iroquois, the St. Lawrence was very different from what I saw yesterday. A tempestuous wind was blowing, the waters were clear and green as those of the ocean despite the night's torrential rain, and hurled our frail craft from one wave to another. We went under sail, although we shipped water from time to time which warned us of our recklessness, but we were afraid of missing the departure of the steamer.

On the contrary, it was she that made us wait and I profited by it to make the acquaintance of the village of Lachine where we were. It's largely composed of country-houses, where they come from Montreal to pass the summer months and to bathe in the St. Lawrence. We started off and soon we saw the river rolling rapidly in pitches of foam. In this area it is split up into various opposite directions by shoals of rocks which act as enormous natural barriers. In the hollows, forming a sort of tortuous channel, the waters meet each other in fury, coming from all directions and leaping in waves so high that we were splashed. It was into this that our pilots hardily launched our fragile bark.

Sometimes, shot like an arrow, almost the whole stern came out of the water; suddenly we saw in front of us a gigantic stratum of rock rearing up. The mill race, suddenly arrested in its course, turns brusquely and boils with swirling waters. It seems as if the end has come; that nothing can now save us from catastrophe. Already the water foaming from the walls splashes in our faces, when, suddenly obeying the impulse of the rudder, our boat rolls on her side and is swallowed in the foam flooded channel. Scarcely are we emerged from this chaos when we came out into Lake George, where the river, throwing wide its banks, soon takes a smooth course.

Next we pass through the Victoria Bridge, the pride of Montreal. It's two miles long and made of iron; 24 piers of stone support it. Then we disembark at a canal by which the same steamers which do the river-run go up stream again, as one can only run the rapids coming down. I felt a real joy at seeing Montreal once more, and, what is very unusual, I did not have to change the impressions made by my first stay there.

ICE CASTLES AT MONTREAL. "The ice, two or three feet thick, is cut into blocks like cut stone and in the winter of 1882-1883 they employed it to build a superb palace, of which photographs are available, where they held a magnificent ball on skates."

Next day I perambulated all the sections of the town that I had not seen. If I could tell you all the religious buildings I encountered on my way, not only would you be surprised, but certainly you would not believe me. Montreal is truly the town of churches. The most magnificently represented religion is the Catholic. Among all the others, Notre Dame (the "French Cathedral"), the church of the Jesuits, and that of our Lady of Lourdes indicate by their sumptuous interiors the riches and power of the French-Canadian Catholics. The number of convents is incalculable. Half the city and surroundings belong to various orders of religion. From Caughnawaga one can see on the opposite bank two superb convents of nuns. Before passing Victoria Bridge one sees another perched on the flank of Mount Royal, on the other side of the park, whose spires and buildings show up against the sky in magnificent silhouette. Beyond the bridge, and in order to reach the landing, we pass an island covered with beautiful trees, also the property of another convent. Finally, from the Windsor Hotel which is altogether outside the centre of the town, I saw from my window, on the second story only, no less than 16 church towers. Hence, it is a saying in Montreal that one could not throw a stone without breaking a church window.

I went back to admire the harbour again where soon all movement would cease. It's very cold in Canada and the winter comes in early. Generally, shipping is stopped from November on, for, in spite of its immensity, the St. Lawrence freezes over and freezes so hard that they were able to build a railway on the ice to cross over it below Victoria Bridge. One result is that many labourers are out of work and they employ them on a veritable mining of the river. The ice, two or three feet thick, is cut into blocks like cut stone and in the winter of 1882-1883[41] they employed it to build a superb palace, of which photographs are available, where they held a magnificent ball on skates.

I learned all these interesting details one evening at dinner with my friends on Dorchester Street. The following day I was to leave for Toronto and Niagara.

At first one is surprised that it isn't higher,
that it isn't bigger, and that one is not
amazed by its immensity.

3

Toronto and Niagara

NEXT day I took the Grand Trunk Railway and a few strokes of the engine-pistons took me away from the old French territory into English Canada. We were soon in the province of Ontario, and we travelled all day before arriving at Toronto. They had coupled a dining car to the rear of the train, where I had lunch and dinner. They serve you at a fixed price, but the menu is abundantly varied and you can have a number of dishes for 75 cents, which is three francs, seventy-five centimes in our money.

I attentively watched the country we passed through. It is an immense plain which seems very fertile and where farming enjoys every advantage. One sees long rows of apple trees in the fields, as in Normandy. It is an unpardonable forgetfulness on my part not to have mentioned a variety of apple called "Marvellous" in the preceding chapter. It's a juicy little apple I was given to eat in Montreal. It's a variety only found in Canada, among 25 or 30 different species, most of which have been acclimatized in France.

From time to time, we approached the St. Lawrence and could see it between masses of trees. It seemed always immense with its high and low islands, big and little, like ships of all sizes in a powerful fleet—there is one area they call the "Thousand Islands" where there are many more than the name indicates (about 1,800 I have been told). Some are mere rocks, other are huge and covered with woods where they hunt rabbits. Soon we arrive at Kingston. In this city, situated on Lake Ontario at the run-out of the river, the main military force of the Dominion is concentrated. Built in 1783 on the site of the French Fort Frontenac, Kingston was, before Ottawa, the capital of Canada and is still an important place. We arrived at the Queen's Hotel in Toronto at midnight. Founded in 1793, Toronto is the biggest city in Ontario and has 80,000 inhabitants. It is situated on the shore of the lake on the north bank and towards the western end.

Next morning I had nothing more urgent than to get a ticket for Niagara. They gave me one all the way to New York and for an unlimited time. In America, the railways are convenient and cheap. Baggage up to 200 pounds is free; but on the point of punctuality I must take back my praise. At Quebec we were two and a half hours late and they said "Wait 'til you go to Toronto!" The Grand Trunk line isn't like the Intercolonial. It starts and arrives on time. But last night, when guiding me to the omnibus for the Queen's Hotel, the conductor's first words were "Two and a half hours late! It's the same every night."

Having checked my bags for the Falls, I began my survey of the town where I had to stay for several hours. I went first to the Zoological Gardens. It's a group of dirty old sheds in which are penned a number of wild animals and birds, the same as in all menageries. There is, however, a magnificent Russian bear that they have not forgotten to call "Peter the Great."

The town is well-built; the streets are straight and wide. There are many fine houses and, all along King Street, very good shops. I noticed a number of imposing-looking churches; but they were almost all closed except one, the Catholic cathedral. It is Gothic in style and decorated with paintings on the inside. It is the type of church you find all over Canada. As for Lake Ontario, the town being on a flat site, one can't see it anywhere and I would have doubted as to its vicinity if I hadn't seen it from the window of my room. There is nothing else very remarkable. The banks are flat and the lake extends its colourless waters out of sight until, at the horizon, they trace a faint line as straight and long as a dead sea.

In a house on an island, which was given him by the City of Toronto, there lives the celebrated Hanlan.[42] This remarkable man is a great citizen whom the Republic has rewarded with gifts such as were given to heroes by a fatherland they had saved. This man, what is he and what has he done? It's only a few years ago that he came back to Toronto, returning from England, and the people in delirium harnessed themselves to his triumphant carriage to draw him along in glory. In a competition on the Thames, Hanlan the Great had beaten the most famous oarsmen of the world, even the Australians, and a grateful

Athens had crowned him as illustrious and built him a temple! This individual, whom one should hear described by experts—for he knew the length of each of his muscles—amassed more than a million in successful bets. The happy proportion of his limbs, we were told, allowed him to guide the movements of his boat with such automatic precision that no one could fight against him. So, Toronto has its Great Man.

I was in too much of a hurry to see the cataract that I knew was so close to me, to prolong my stay in Toronto, besides there was nothing interesting to hold me. In America, there are only two things for a traveller to see. The appearance of the country and next the customs, the business and the politics of the people.

NED HANLAN. "It's only a few years ago that he came back to Toronto, returning form England, and the people in delirium harnessed themselves to his triumphant carriage to draw him along in glory."

Unlike countries where civilization is many centuries old, there are not the thousand memories and the thousand ruins of antiquity to seek. I left, then, that day.

In the evening I arrived at Niagara Falls at 6:25, the time listed. It was snowing a little. It was the first snow of the winter and the first of November. It was black night. A few rickety old coaches waited in the shadows, their drivers hurling the names of hotels at the travellers all at the same time. It's no small embarrassment when going to the Falls to decide what house to go to and whether to choose the American or Canadian side, the more so at this season as many hotels are closed, the summer season being over and the winter season—during which one comes to admire the waterfalls partly frozen over—not yet come.

Very fortunately, my friends from Dorchester Street had thought of everything and, following their advice, I alighted at the Hotel Rosli on the Canadian side.[43] In my turn, I would strongly recommend anyone going to this place to knock at the same door. It is less a hotel than a furnished house where you can be sure of the honesty of the host and where they greet you in a polite and friendly fashion.

Mr. Rosli, a great big Swiss, came forward to receive me very civilly and brought me to my room and then invited me to have tea. When I wrote my name in the register and he saw that I was French, he spoke to me in my own language. He kept me company at the table and served excellent food. They had recommended him to me at Montreal saying "he is a splendid cook and will save you money." On his own, he undertook to arrange everything for the morrow's journey and to set the fare with the driver.

On this assurance I went tranquilly to bed, a little overcome by the thought that I was soon to find myself face to face with one of the most magnificent sights in the world. I was at least half a mile from the Falls and I could hear their murmuring through the closed shutters. It sounded as if there was a river dam just below the hotel. Next morning at nine o'clock, I got in the carriage to start my excursion.

Sometimes, during one of those nights when the stars burn with unusual brilliance in the black heavens, I have been in the habit of watching one of them but concentrating on it all the fullness of my attention. I reunited in my gaze, so to speak, every quivering bit of life in me. I made a violent effort to distil all my powers of imagination in one small compass. Then I could see only this one star, alone in the heavens. Little by little, its light diminished and it seemed that I was drawn up towards it across the vastness of space. All of a sudden, I was truly aware of the immense and infinite void. I passed through, to the end, the immeasurable distance which separated me from it, and for a second I saw it as it was, in all its globular grandeur, rolling its fabulous world in the immeasurable depths of nothing—and then it was only the flicker of an apparition that with all the power of my will I was able to conjure up; and that disappeared suddenly as soon as my imagination failed. At first sight, I always found the star beautiful; it was only afterwards it appeared as it really was: terrifying!

I beg the reader's pardon for this digression; but there is no other way in which I could better make him understand the disappointment that one feels at the first sight of the Falls of Niagara. It is not what one has seen in dreams, and for the reason, precisely, that our soul is too shallow to imagine marvels that it has not seen, except as monstrosities.

At first one is surprised that it isn't higher, that it isn't bigger, and that one is not amazed by its immensity. For all that it is really high, it's really big, and one's eyes see it as it is; but our soul cannot understand because it is not geared to such conceptions. One must give it time to adjust and to see at last in this blinding light. To do it properly, one should go away and not return for

THE ROSLI HOTEL, BRIDGE STREET, NIAGARA FALLS. "It is less a hotel than a furnished house where you can be sure of the honesty of the host and where they greet you in a polite and friendly fashion."

a month. These are not only my own impressions that I give here, but those of everyone who has been to Niagara and who, disappointed the first time, have been overcome with wonder on returning. Many people, besides, have warned me of the disenchantment that awaited me, but I didn't believe them.

I was not, therefore, seized with stupefaction, when I suddenly beheld the cataract, nor when I got out of the carriage on the bank of the Canadian falls, with the American falls facing me. It is an immense river that hurls itself over there, in one single leap, rolling noisily from a height of 160 feet on a width of over 200; and I have read that, every second, 28,000 tons of water passes over.

I continued on. I wanted to see everything and buy at any price the delicious sensation that would come from being familiar with such a great spectacle. Starting out in dull and overcast weather, I was lucky enough soon to be favoured with the presence of the sun. I climbed into the observatory, from which one can see the Canadian falls whose semi-circular shape has earned the name of Horseshoe Falls. I donned a sailor's oilskins to go down the cliff, and there, clinging to the wet wall of the rock, I saw the deluge passing over my head and its thunder growling at my feet. Saved from the elements, I went into the shops where I became the prey of some pretty girls who emptied my pockets to fill them with souvenirs. I stopped at the Burning Spring where the waters burn like the flames of Hell; at Three Sisters Island, where the great trees shake their manes of creepers above the rapids which boil furiously upstream from the cataract, I passed on to Goat Island whose rocks are heaped up between the Horseshoe Falls on the one side and the American falls on the other; from which the water arcs in a single jet in a straight line. I went down to the foot of the island, where I was inundated by a moist spray, and where it began to appear to me that the water falls very strongly and from a great height. I then left the United States to re-enter Canada and I crossed Niagara below the falls on a wire cable bridge more than two hundred feet long, which is suspended more than 250 feet above the river. This has hardly made its leap but it flows peaceable and limpid in its rock-bordered bed.

I have one thing left to visit; these are the terrible Whirlpool Rapids where the unfortunate Captain Webb met his death.[44] They are three miles below the falls. There, one is immediately seized with fright at the spectacle of the torrent which threshes its waves perpetually in all directions; the whole St. Lawrence passes through here.

I had seen everything and I went back to get my things together and take some notes. I was to leave for New York at eight o'clock that night, but I wished to see the cataract again before leaving, and I went there on foot towards the end of the evening. Instead of following my first route and arriving at the same level as the top of the falls, I took a road that dropped to the bottom of the ravine where the Niagara flows.

I went to the edge of the water, waiting until I got there before looking. Then, blocking the horizon, the cataract with its twin falls appeared to me in all its sublime magnificence. I took note of its colossal proportions; I could not go back with my deceptive first impressions. I at last understood this marvel, which had never ceased spreading itself before me, and that, in spite of everything, I had such trouble in appreciating. It is unique in the world and it is beautiful, that's all.

But who could ever describe this prodigious mass of water, foaming in rapids and smashing into a gulf whence it escapes in white spray flung to the heavens and then flowing further on without a ripple? Who could describe the fairy look of this cataract which seems, in the sun, an avalanche of snow across which fugitive rainbows sported in the breeze? And that island of goats on whose heaped-up rocks, great trees stretched their mossy arms, moistened incessantly by American and Canadian waters.

CAPTAIN MATTHEW WEBB. "I have only one thing left to visit; these are the terrible Whirlpool Rapids where the unfortunate Captain Webb met his death."

As the sun was about to disappear and I thought of returning, a ray from its setting flared upon the American side, enveloping in a rose-coloured tint the cloud of vapour that rose from the Canadian Falls. The sky, everywhere else covered with thick clouds, spread already on the earth the early shades of evening. This trail of fire seemed a pathway of light by which poetry descended from the heavens and filled with solemn sadness the sublime beauties of these places. In such moments, how little and isolated one feels; how the heart overflows with emotion and fills with a thousand dear memories. How strongly one would love if one were in love!

I stayed thus, plunged in a sad contemplation, until all light had gone. Then I went away in haste from those places, where it seemed that nothingness was advancing to seize me, and I returned, my soul full of sorrow. It is surely a great spectacle that puts a man in such an ecstasy!

It is a mark of the Yankee character to affect contempt for those they serve. This applies to employees of all classes, as if we should be humbly grateful for the honour they deign to confer on us by accepting our money.

4

NEW YORK AND A RETURN TO FRANCE

AFTER passing the night in a sleeping car and having followed during the morning the lovely valley of the Delaware with its woods tapestried with rhododendrons, I finally arrived at New York. Before arrival, an employee passes through the train and for a dollar and a half gives out tickets for the "ferry": namely, the transport of your bags and yourself in one of these conveyances called "transfer wagons."

New York, capital of the state of the same name, is the biggest city on the American continent. It occupies the greater part of Manhattan Island, situated at the mouth of the Hudson. This river flows round the city to the west while an arm of the sea called the East River separates it from Long Island. Across from New York, on Long Island, is Brooklyn, Williamsburg and other places that one should think of as suburbs of the great city, as well as Jersey City and Hoboken, which are on the left bank of the Hudson.

The port of NewYork is one of the finest in the world. Its entry, at Sandy Hook, is 18 miles from the southern end of the island of Manhattan. New York was founded in 1614 by the Dutch, who called it New Amsterdam. Its name was changed to New York when it fell to the British in 1664. At that time, it had scarcely 2000 inhabitants. It has today a population of 942,377 souls and counting the suburbs, 1,500,000.[45]

Streets encumbered with packing-cases, with drays, with goods of all sorts, this is what one painfully traverses on the way from the wharf. The elevated railroad, running on each side of the avenue at the height of the first story, succeeds in giving a most desperately mercantile aspect to this part of the town and makes one think it one vast warehouse. To complete the picture, the wires for the telegraph, telephone, and electric light, cross and intertwine and entangle with each other so thickly that they seem like a net held over the streets, for fear that at night a few rays might fall from the stars on the pavement.

One soon comes out on Broadway, the great artery of New York, which cuts the town in two for its whole length. It's the street of shops, stores and restaurants. A busy street, but too straight, where one goes for a promenade between four and six in the afternoon on the left side of the street, as one would on the right side of the Champs-Elysées, in Paris.

Fifth Avenue goes along both sides of Madison Square where it cuts Broadway diagonally. With its master-mansions, its vast hotels and its numerous churches of all religions, it is the largest, the most beautiful, and the most aristocratic, of the streets of the Empire City. There, all commerce has ceased. A few very rare shops, among which is a branch of Goupil's.[46] There is not a single house in Paris that could be reproduced here and be considered in the first rank.

If one tried to establish a comparison between the two capitals (for New York is really the capital of the United States), one could say that 5th Avenue resembles at its best the Boulevard Malherbes; no crowds, no shops, fine carriages and rich homes. But shortly, beyond Madison Square, 5th Avenue takes an original cast because of a range of splendid hotels (The Brunswick, the Windsor, etc.) and because of a number of churches of all types, among which the most beautiful is the Catholic cathedral, a modern building, superbly Gothic in style.

Before seeing all that, I had got off at the Hotel Denis on Broadway. They had recommended it to me, but this time I will refrain from doing the like to the readers for whom I am writing. On going to my room, I asked for my bags and I was assured that they would follow me in moment. It was early and I counted on having the time to dress, to lunch and to go to the Italian Opera where Capoul and Nilsson were singing.[47] I wished also to profit by having spare time before I made calls on some persons I knew at New York; I was looking forward to an afternoon of no responsibilities that I was reserving for myself.

But by now it was already noon and no word of my bags: I rang. A young servant girl came and asked me in an impertinent tone what I wanted. "My bags, of course," I said. It was the second time I had asked for them. They replied that they would send them up. At the end of half an hour, still nothing! I lean once more on the bell-push, and a third specimen of domestic presents herself. Same question, same answer, same wait.

Rendered impatient, I took the course of going to the desk to find out what all this meant. They tell me that my bags have not yet arrived from the station, and they add ironically that they may not before night. I was furious but what could I do.

What annoyed me the most were these three servants who successively came to me and who, instead of telling me that my bags had not arrived, had left me vainly waiting. But in America all the hotel personnel, managers and valets, are crude and unhelpful and the only way of not suffering from them is to act as they do. These gentlemen are very shocked if one seems to treat them as inferiors. I had already made this observation on the railway, where the employees seat themselves next to you without embarrassment and speak to you as if you were a comrade…which doesn't prevent them accepting a tip for giving a bit of information.

Briefly, it was past three o'clock when my bags turned up and I had been in New York since 11 in the morning. One more complaint to make against the railway companies of the United States. It is a mark of the Yankee character to affect contempt for those they serve. This applies to employees of all classes, as if we should be humbly grateful for the honour they deign to confer on us by accepting our money.

Once outside the hotel, I found that I was in a good spot and just at the right time to find the whole town on the sidewalks. I came back after lounging around for two hours, and if I was then asked what I thought of New York, I could scarcely express my opinion except on the New York girls. Well, I can say to the girls of Paris, without trying to flatter them, that they can be easy. I saw many lovely costumes, many well turned-out women, but I have no memory of anyone really beautiful. Certainly charm, if not beauty, has not failed to hold its court with us. There is only one Paris in the world and Parisiennes only in Paris.

Actually, there is very little to see at New York, and if one is not in business the life is terribly monotonous. Eight days is more than is needed to note the customs and habits of the inhabitants and discover whatever there is of originality. As for politics and business, I say nothing of them. In all countries they can be the subject of long and learned studies, but I hold them to be taboo things that I will keep from touching except by chance. Neither do I undertake to bring my readers anywhere except to bars, theatres, promenades and other places of the same kind.

I passed my first evening alone at Niblo's Garden. They presented "Excelsior," the famous ballet that the Eden Theatre had introduced at Paris. What can I say of it today that would be of any interest? Everyone has seen it or heard it discussed. Everyone knows what a revolution it has caused, by the effects in the ensemble, in the art of French choreography and what controversy it has also raised among folk of great ability, on the subject of stage presentation. This last observation will cause me to say a few words on the stage setting of "Excelsior" at New York.

The Americans praised "Brooklyn Bridge" highly. That can be understood as patriotic enthusiasm. And even I can give thanks to the authors for this spectacle. But as for the others, I will wager that M. Sarcy himself would not be pleased with them. The hall is spacious and I was far from the stage. In spite of that, the daubing of the scenery did not seem any less crude and primitive. First, there was a complete lack of manner, space and illusion; next, a lack of taste, a lack of finish and a lack of imagination. For example, there is one scene where a curtain is shown on which is painted, in a sort of apotheosis, the busts of the heroes who illustrate the ballet. The work of this is so barbarous that I dare not even compare this canvas to those that serve as sign boards for the yokels at a country fair. There was one particular naked woman who, instead of being lightly enveloped in some poetically coloured swathing, which could alone excuse her presence, seemed as if cut out of a sheet of zinc and daubed in with charcoal. The Americans applauded this!

And note that the New York theatres are no mere tenth-raters. One can hear there every winter the masterpieces of literature and of music, presented by the most celebrated artists of the entire world. It is because of this that I would wish the setting were more worthy of the people it encloses.

All these comments serve only to make this character analysis; the Americans lack taste from the artistic viewpoint, as they lack polish on the social side. To support my statement I will quote an undeniable fact. A magnificent Sèvres vase of royal blue and gilded bronze has been donated for a charity lottery by M. Grevy. The person who won it thought nothing of it "because it was all one colour" and sold it to a dealer where it remained a long time unsold. It is held in contempt. Finally, a friend in whose home I was received with all the grace in the world, found it and bought it for a price much below its real value. I got this story from himself. He told it to me when I was admiring the vase which, placed on a pedestal, made a superb ornament for his drawing room.

Besides, it is only on the majority of Americans that I mean to impose this indictment. There are exceptions there as everywhere. But they are very numerous and the proof of this is that there are hardly any works of art in America except those imported from foreign lands. It may be said that in buying them thus they show proof of good taste. I'm not too sure, and what leaves me in doubt is the enormous and popular development in this country of chromolithography, which for me is the antithesis of art. Besides, many men who are wealthy or vain, collect for display masterpieces of painting or rare editions of which they are absolutely incapable of appreciating the beauties.

These, then, were my first impressions of Washington's fatherland. But charming friends soon took it on themselves to allay my bitterness. They were greatly surprised to see me and no less great was my pleasure at being so well received. During my whole stay, there was nothing but invitations to lunch and dinner and I found enough delights in this house to change my opinion of all America.

Without them, what would I have done all by myself for 10 days in New York? One could see a few picture galleries, but I have little doubt that the best there is in that line is to be found in the bar of the Hoffman Hotel. In this hall, where one drinks, the walls were hung with pictures by Bouguereau and Correggio and with Gobelin tapestries and with Indian, Japanese, and Chinese works of art. The waiters' napkins hang on marble Venuses. The pipe-smoke disappears in the folds of oriental hangings and the electric light falling from the candelabras fills with pearls the glasses where the champagne is sparkling.

Of all I saw in New York, it is that which seemed to me most worthy of a visit, for, of its kind, it is certainly unique in the world. Such a setup would seem strange in this place if I did not add that there, the idlers spend their existence mostly in the lobbies and the bars of hotels. During the day they come in there at all hours for a brush-up or a shoe-shine; to tidy their clothing or to buy theatre tickets; or to consult the hotel register. It is at the same time the convenience and the amusement of everybody.

As one may see, it is not much with which to occupy one's existence and so the great part of people are in business. Besides, it is only the business man that is respected and there, where the aristocracy of blood does not exist, that of wealth is all powerful. My friends, whom I often went to see in their office on Beaver Street, are agents for the champagne firm of Piper Heidsieck and other great brands of French wines. Along with Mumm and Roederer, the champagne they represent is the most highly thought-of in New York and the agents of these three firms do a huge volume of business. It's unbelievable how much of this type of wine is consumed in America. One tires of it quickly and one sighs for a good glass of Bordeaux; but even in the best places it is very dear without being good.

There are some French restaurants where they serve you a *vin ordinaire* that is much better. One day, when I was tired of lunching on coffee-with-cream and ice water, I entered one of these establishments and had a singular encounter. It was on 26th Street, for, as one knows, all the streets of New York intersect at right angles and are numbered except in the older part of the town. The waiter who served me, observing that I was French, told me that he was French also. I was alone in the room at the time and he started conversing with me.

He started by telling me that he was not using his own name and could not tell it to me. This was out of pride, for he was an old French army officer, a captain of infantry. He is only 40 years old and has been here five years. He came out to try his luck after resigning his commission, saw his hopes disappointed and had to seek a place to live. He had been in Mexico as a cook on an American warship and had not the slightest notion of the culinary art. However, justifying the proverb, he got out of his troubles by his French wit. When he got back, he took the job where I met him. He told me that the situation of a waiter is very different in New York from what it is in Paris. "First," he said, "we are altogether independent. Next, we are paid. We get a dollar a day and make twice as much again in tips." He told me after, that he was not the only one in New York in this fix. He knew several French officers managing their livelihood in the same manner as himself; the head waiter was a one-time big businessman from Hamburg.

Germans are there in crowds. It is an invasion. They have their own theatre where they put on German plays in the German language; they have their own political meetings, and their Representatives who form an imposing party in the Assembly; and they have their newspapers in their own language. They have great halls in the better parts of the town where they drink beer in unison while listening to German music. They have restaurants, hairdressers; indeed, if things keep up, they will have everything. And I have not spoken of the hundred thousand Jews who, after their fashion, work high and low in money matters.

As far as invasions are concerned, I prefer the Italian. New York thinks likewise for they have built two palaces to receive them. One is called the Academy of Music, and the other the Italian Metropolitan Opera. During my stay, Patti reigned in the first and Nilsson was enthroned in the second.[48] The Metropolitan, although not finished on the outside, had just been opened. And they were very anxious to know which would have the greater success over its rival.

The evening I went to the Academy of Music it was for a Premiere...so called because "The Thieving Magpie" (*La Gazza Ladra*) which was being given had not been played in New York for 30 years, and also because Patti, who had just arrived, was making her seasonal debut that evening.

I was in the orchestra stalls; and as these are much sought after by the ladies as by the men, I couldn't have been better placed to see the house. All around me were the most elegant costumes; a robe of pale blue covered by a veil of white lace; a robe of white Flemish silk trimmed with gold. Plumes held in place in the hair by diamond pins. In a word, everything that the most refined luxury could produce. A superb programme was distributed free, which indicated what pieces were to be given during the season by "Her Majesty's Opera Company," for this troupe in which Adeline Patti plays is that of the Queen of England.

At eight o'clock the orchestra struck up the overture. Good technique, but nonetheless inferior to what one hears in Paris at the Opera or the Opera Comique. When Patti came on stage, there was a storm of applause, 10 rounds at least. All she could do was bow and smile in the most gracious fashion. Beautiful, she looks only 20 years old behind the footlights. As soon as they allowed her, she sang the cavatina "Di piacer mi balza il cor," which is both the opening number and the most brilliant selection in the opera. She is an excellent comedian and an admirable singer. She carries this delicate music with a miraculously light touch; she sings with incomparable style, expression, and delicacy; and with both art and artlessness. But it is, of course, superfluous to say this to those who know her and useless to say it to those who don't. It would be impossible to count the number of bouquets, flower arrangements, etc. with which they overpowered, rather than greeted, the Diva.

All I can say is that after the first and last act, the actors had to form a chain to store the presents in the corridors, and after bows and smiles, Patti threw kisses to the enthusiastic audience.

Between the acts I vainly sought to discover some beauty among this elite of the great world of New York. I saw beautiful costumes, marvellous diamonds, but not one lovely face. This would have left me with a very sad impression of American girls if I had not fortunately encountered two ravishing blondes at the exit, two blondes with golden hair and brown eyes whom I ventured to admire at my leisure.

If, after this evening and that which I passed at the Metropolitan Opera, I had to give judgment in favour of one or other of these theatres, I would certainly give preference to the former.

It is true that I am very out of date for my century. I am not a Wagnerian and it was precisely Lohengrin that I saw played at the Metropolitan; and sung by Signor Campaninim while Nilsson did Elsa. Indeed, excellent as they are as singers, these two artists are nonetheless mediocre comedians and, besides, one feels that both of them have voices that are a bit worn out. Indeed, it is very rare to preserve the freshness of a voice as long as Patti. Also, my main complaint is that, several times, the conductor was obliged to interrupt both the choir and the orchestra in a loud voice. This shocked me terribly. But I know of no theatre where one is so comfortably seated as in this one. Doubtless it was specially constructed for hearing Wagner and precautions were consequently taken. One could easily sleep in one's seat without troubling one's neighbour.

If I add to the names of these illustrious actors those of Capoul, who sang at the Metropolitan also, and Irving, the great English tragedian that I had applauded in "The Merchant of Venice," it will be admitted that I was speaking truth when I say that the most celebrated artists of the entire world can be heard every winter in the Empire City.

(Note: Since I wrote these lines, which make me blush today, and which I leave in solely for my mortification, my ears have been opened and I have been converted to Wagner. It's mostly to Mr. Alfred Ernst's well executed work on Berlioz that I owe the delayed pleasure of having appreciated this genius).

If I continue this chapter thus, one would believe that there is nothing but theatres to see at New York. In that case, brave reader, it may now be opportune to come with me in a promenade that I made with my friend, the owner of the Sèvres vase.

ADELINA PATTI. "She is an excellent comedian and an admirable singer. She carries this delicate music with a miraculously light touch."

The object of our journey was a visit to Brooklyn, the home of his grand-parents. We stopped first at the post office. Following the American custom, each has his own box with a key, so that he can get or send for his letters when-ever he wishes. There are also postmen for those who don't have boxes, but most people prefer the first arrangement since the deliveries are not reliable.

Naturally politics is the cause, for, in the United States, perhaps more than in any other republic, each new Representative indulges his friends with the posts previously enjoyed by the *protégés* of his predecessor. Because of this, it is impossible to have employees who know their business. When they are in place, they know they can hold it by influence, and they care for nothing else. Politics is even more powerful in America than in France. Election days are feast days; the shops are closed, business is postponed, and when they have voted they spend the rest of the time in amusement.

Although I have no desire to launch upon a long dissertation on this sub-ject, I can't refrain from saying a word on the parties of the United States. There are two principal ones, the Democrats and the Republicans. The latter are violently committed to central government and want a Republic centered on Washington; the former have a contrary programme of enlarging the inde-pendence of the states. They also propose that only gold and silver money shall circulate, although they use mostly only paper. Banknotes of from one to five dollars are the ordinary currency.

Talking all the while, and exhausting our guide of information, we soon came to the famous Brooklyn Bridge, on which we were to cross. While I am very skeptical with regard to the eighth wonder of the world—there are so many places where they show it to you—I am tempted to say that I have found it here and that Brooklyn Bridge is it. It is impossible to describe it. All I have heard or read of it doesn't give the least idea of it and a drawing or photograph is no help to better understanding. One must be up on it to see from above the high buildings flattened out and the ships passing beneath you; the enormous iron cables that support the bridge; the two roads for carriages that run on each side; the lines of the parapet; the two lines of railway running themselves on the inside of each road; and these two railroads separated in their turn by a space of equal size for the passage of the telegraph and telephone lines that connect New York to Brooklyn, and finally in the centre of the bridge above the electric lines, the footway for pedestrians. The trains do not go by steam but are drawn by a chain as the route has a steep double slope. At night, everything is illuminated by electric light. Briefly, it is a prodigy of science and skill before which one falls down in admiration. It is not a bridge, it is a monument and I don't hesitate to pronounce it the finest one in New York.

After a six-minute drive in a carriage, one lands on the other side in a great provincial city of 500,000 inhabitants. It's no longer New York, the capital, the Empire City. There are no longer these vast hotels like cities in themselves. No more sources of electric light for the streets and squares; not even any elevated railways such as transport travelers from one end of New York to the other, in the air, for 10 cents. It is true they are talking of erecting a line. But it's not the less pleasant for being less striking. First, the cost of living is from 25 to 30 per cent less than on the other side of the water. Next, there is a magnificent park where the grey squirrels jump about and nibble on the very walks. There is a cemetery where they bring tourists because of its picturesque qualities. There is also a fine street lined with trees, gardens and villas, called Clinton Avenue, and which is the "Rue Passy" of New York. Many rich people live there in retirement from business.

My friend's grandparents lived on Clinton Avenue. May they know how touched I was, on being presented, to find that I was not a stranger in this house and that my name was well-known to them. By five o'clock we were back in my friend's home, on Park Avenue—one of the finest in New York. After dinner we went for a moment to the Casino. The Moorish Room is by far the handsomest in New York. The curtain, which opens in the middle, is blue velvet decked out with embroidery; I have never seen anything in this line so sumptuous. They play operettas in this theatre. This evening, being a Sunday, they gave a concert. They have become less strict there than in Old England. The hall was full and these Lord's Day congregations, which would not have been tolerated a few years ago, are now very much in favour.

It is thus that I passed the eve of my departure. There was nothing interesting left for me to see at New York so I decided to pack my bags. I had already reserved my cabin on the *Labrador* of the Transatlantic Company, and I had taken my ticket for Paris. I wished to buy some books for the voyage. I stopped in front of a bookshop where were displayed the latest novels appearing in Paris. Imagine my astonishment to find them priced at $1.45 (7 fr.25), for a volume worth 3 fr.50! It is thus with all foreign publications and is caused by an unreasonable tax. Many Americans protest this, claiming that it greatly obstructs the development of education.

Finally the 14th of November arrives. In leaving New York we could watch the marvellous sight of the roadstead for a long time. From far away, the Brooklyn Bridge gave a magic effect. I won't go into details of description; everyone knows that this place is considered one of the most beautiful in the world, and it is hard to add anything to that.

During all the crossing we were terribly knocked about by the storm; but on the second night after our departure particularly, a furious tempest attacked our ship. Thanks to her resistance to all tests and to the courage of our commander, we escaped. It was not without paying a tribute to the sea. At a moment when they were least expecting it, a huge sea rose in front, so high that it put out the mizzen-mast light, and falling on the bridge in one great mass, smashed the Captain's cabin and several sailors, two of whom were crushed to pieces. It was at night and the Master of the ship was in bed, not being on watch. At this stroke, he leaped from his couch thinking the ship had broken in two. I got these details from the commander himself. Besides, when I reached Paris, the news of the event had preceded us and those who had friends on board were not too sure what had happened to them.

I hadn't seen France for 18 months when at last, having left Le Havre on the Boat Train, I soon got down at St. Lazare station. During the day, while making my first tour of the boulevards, I met one of the *Labrador*'s passengers and I cried out, reaching him my hand…

"New World. Good bye! Paris is more beautiful than anything else I've seen!"

ENDNOTES

1 The photo from which the drawing of Lucretia Stabb was made can be found on page 372, Vol. 5 of *The Book of Newfoundland*. Her name was on the back of de la Chaume's drawing and as Miss White noted, "the Stabb family was well known in St. John's at that time." It is likely she was the daughter of H. J. Stabb, a merchant and insurance agent who was also "consular agent for the Kingdom of Italy."

2 De la Chaume's drawing of St. John's Harbour first appeared in *The Newfoundland Quarterly* 70.3 (1974):12.

3 Perlin wrote about the de la Chaume translation in his "Wayfarer' column, "A Gallic Glance at Nfld.," *Daily News*, January 4, 1962, p. 4.

4 All the observations about de la Chaume's description of the seal fishery are contained in a letter from Shannon Ryan to Robin McGrath, September 17, 1997.

5 Letter from Dr. James M. F. McGrath to Premier J.R. Smallwood, July 20, 1961, included with the manuscript of "Newfoundland: The Land and It's [sic] Ladies" deposited in the Centre for Newfoundland Studies.

6 Letter from Mary M. White to Dr. James M.F. McGrath, October 15, 1970.

7 "Emile and Henri de la Chaume: Vice-Consul and Trade Attaché Respectively for France in St. John's, Newfoundland from 1 June 1882 to 19 October 1883." *The Newfoundland Quarterly* 70.3 (1974):12-16.

8 This reference is probably to former Prime Minister of the Colony, Sir Frederick Bowker Terrington Carter, who had been made Chief Judge in 1880. If there is no Governor (or, today, Lieutenant Governor) then the Chief Judge steps into his shoes as a constitutional convention. Carter was probably filling in for Governor Maxse at the time of de la Chaume's arrival in the Colony. Maxse spent much of the time as governor of Newfoundland residing in Germany. Carter received his knighthood in 1878, the first Newfoundlander to be so honoured.

9 According to Paul O'Neill, soprano Clara Fisher was "the doyenne of musical circles" in St. John's for almost ten years. She lived with her mother on the west side of Cochrane Street, and performed in a series of light opera hits, produced and directed by Charles Hutton, before returning to Boston where she resumed her American career.

10 Fr. Galveston is a *nom de geurre*. Archivist Larry Dohey suggests that Father Galveston was probably Michael Francis Howley, later Archbishop Howley. Like Galveston, Howley was related to Father John St. John by marriage, he spoke French and Italian, and while he was not actually an

artist, he loved to doodle and a number of documents in the Roman Catholic Archives are decorated with his sketches of people. The drawing reproduced here identifies the subject as "The Steward, alias cook, alias Tom, alias Paddy 'Mara." Howley writes in his diary aboard the brigantine *Glance,* en route to Scotland in 1853 that "I have taken a portrait of him from life that you will find on the last page of this journal and I believe it to be understood that I positively assert it to be no caricature, the only fault being (they all say) that it is too handsome! He is a native of Kilkenny but left it when he was a boy. Since then he has spent many years in the cod fishery of Newfoundland but he has also seen a fair deal of the world, whether he went as a sailor or cook I don't know."

[11] Thomas Joseph Power (1830-1893) was appointed Bishop of St. John's in 1870 after the death of Bishop Mullock. He had a great interest in sacred music and ritual, which obviously appealed to de la Chaume's own interests. Power is buried under the altar of the Basilica.

[12] Stuart Cumberland was the stage name of Charles Garner, a contact mind reader. Cumberland popularized the performance of mind-reading and at the time of de la Chaume's visit to St. John's, was lecturing and debunking so-called "spiritualistic phenomena" on both sides of the Atlantic. He later described how performers achieved their apparent telepathic communication through the use of codes in his 1888 text *Thought-Reader's Thoughts: Being the Impressions and Confessions of Stuart Cumberland.*

[13] Sir William Whiteway was Newfoundland's longest serving Prime Minister prior to Confederation. He was a determined supporter of the railway, and after de la Chaume left Newfoundland he negotiated an agreement to give the French greater access to bait in return for allowing a west coast terminus of the railway.

[14] According to Shannon Ryan, no sealing ship called the *French Shore* ever existed. The *French Shore* is an invention and this whole section is fabricated from other sources. Many of the details of this section are incorrect. McGrath, who went to the ice in 1919 aboard the *Terra Nova,* would have been well aware of the inaccuracies of the descriptions.

[15] Shannon Ryan writes that "the men did not sleep in the 'forecastle' but in the hold back aft where there was by this time a between deck directly over the main hold and pounds which were filled with coal.

[16] Shannon Ryan points out that "The men were not forbidden to wash *per se* but it was pointless to do so and drinking water was scarce—but was replenished from the many pools of water on the ice."

[17] The *Greenland* was a real vessel, sailing out of Carbonear in the 1880s. Shannon Ryan reports that there were no steamer disasters in 1883 or 1884. The *Greenland* lost 48 men in 1894, and the ship itself sank in 1907.

18 "The encounter with the hood seal sounds fictitious," writes Shannon Ryan, "because they were easily killed by two sealers working together—one would hit the seal on the tail and as it reared up its head to turn towards its tormenter, the second sealer would strike it a fatal blow across the throat." Ryan has talked to sealers who claim to have killed a hood single-handed, but they cannot be killed by a blow to the head because of the hood.

19 Henry Berkeley Fitzhardinge Maxse was appointed Governor of Newfoundland in 1881. He was involved in settlement of the French Shore issue, but died in St. John's just a month before de la Chaume left the Colony as a result of the wounds he received during the Battle of Balaclava in the Charge of the Light Brigade.

20 This conversation is imaginary. As the translator put it in a letter to Joseph Smallwood, if de la Chaume "had said to Shea one tenth of what he claims, he would have found himself out on his backside in the mud of Military Road before he had a chance to finish."

21 According to Joan Ritcey of the Centre for Newfoundland Studies, the pamphlet de la Chaume is responding to is probably a 35 page document titled *Report of the Council of the Royal Colonial Institute on the Newfoundland Fishery Question*, November, 1875. Ritcey writes that the name Whitman does not appear anywhere in the institute report but "clearly Whitman's brochure or letter was a summation or discussion of this report."

22 "*La Pêcheries de Terreneuve: droits de la France: exposés aux assertions de l'Institut Colonial*. Quebec, imprimerie de 'L'Évènement' 1876." (H.d.l.C.)

23 "*Geography of Newfoundland, for the use of schools* by J.P. Howley." (H. d.l.C.)

24 The date mentioned here originally read 1883, but a note in the margin of the translator's copy of the manuscript indicates that this date should probably read 1833. The context, which refers to some time in the past, suggests that 1883 was an error and it has been altered to 1833.

25 The judge, identified by de la Chaume as Honorable Carlston, was probably James Gerve Conroy (1836 -1915). In 1882, the year de la Chaume arrived in St. John's, Conroy accepted appointments as Judge of the Central District court and Stipendiary Magistrate, positions he held until his death.

26 "De la Chaume says fifty thousand, but this is absurd."(J.M.McG.)

27 "*Newfoundland, its Fisheries and General Resources*, by Sir A. Shea, K.C.M.G. "(H. d.l.C.)

28 "I have borrowed the technical and statistical details from notes taken from *Newfoundland, the Oldest British Colony* etc. by J. Hatton and Rev. M. Harvey." (H.d.l.C.)

29 Dr. Galveston is almost certainly Thomas Howley (1840-1889), brother of Archbishop Howley (who appears here as Father Galveston). He was a physician in St. John's. Like the translator, Dr. McGrath, he developed an interest in medicine while working for druggist Thomas McMurdo, and then trained as a physician and surgeon in Ireland before returning to Newfoundland. Howley was married to Mary St. John, sister of Father St. John of St. Joseph's Parish, St. Mary's Bay. His photograph, from the Archive of the Roman Catholic Archdioceses of St. John's, has the caption "Dr. Tom Howley, Physician to the Confederate Army," on the front. The reverse has the pencil notation "Poor Tom," suggesting that the subject had died by the time the note was made. Dr. Howley actually served with the 25th United States Coloured Troops, a regiment of black soldiers.

30 "Three hundred and forty miles to Harbour Grace? Henri slipped here." (J. McG.)

31 "See *Newfoundland, the Oldest British Colony*, by J. Hatton and Rev. M. Harvey, London 1883." (H.d.l.C)

32 Albert Perlin wondered how de la Chaume "knew the politicians spoke bad English since he, himself, admitted that on his arrival in St. John's he knew barely three words of the language." "A Gallic Glance at Nfld.," *Daily News*, January 4, 1962, p. 4.

33 Father John St. John was born in St. John's, ordained in Rome and his first pastoral appointment was as curate at St. Mary's, St. Mary's Bay. He was appointed as the first parish priest to St. Joseph's Parish in January of 1875, and held that position for twenty-one years. In 1914, he was named Domestic Prelate by Pope Benedict XV with the title of Monsignor.

34 Lady S. was probably Louisa Boushetta Hart, second wife of Sir Ambrose Shea. Shea was awarded the K.C.M.G. by Queen Victoria while a delegate to the International Fisheries Exhibition in London in 1883, just months before the ball de la Chaume describes. Prince George became George V, as his older brother died while in line of succession.

35 Sister Mary Magdalen O'Shaughnessy (1793-1889) was born in Galway, Ireland and came to Newfoundland with three other Presentation nuns in 1833. At the time of de la Chaume's visit, she was the Superioress of the Convent.

36 Luigi Cherubine (1760-1842) was an Italian-born composer of operas and sacred music. He spent most of his working life in France, and like de la Chaume he was a keen amateur painter. The text of "O Salutaris" is by Thomas Aquinas.

37 "I have not attempted to translate Henri's poetry into English verse." (J. M. McG.)

38 The Honorific letters for Admiral of the Fleet Sir John Edmund Commerell (1829-1901) should probably read V.C., G.C.B. He was awarded the Victoria Cross when he was 26, for action he took during the Crimean War. In 1866, he commanded the *HMS Terrible*, assisting the *Great Eastern* to lay the first successful Atlantic cable.

39 Gerhard Bassler has identified this honorary consul of the German Empire as Robert Henry Prowse, brother of D.W. Prowse who wrote *A History of Newfoudland*. In *Vikings to U-Boats*, Bassler writes that Prowse's extant annual reports to the German foreign office form "a litany of never-ending economic woes" and that he "complains about unsatisfactory fishing seasons, con-flicts with the French over bait caught on the French Shore and high bounties paid by the French government" as well as other difficulties. Bassler suggests that as Prowse moved largely in English social circles, the widows were probably not German.

40 Caughnawaga, now called Kahnawake, is an Iroquois settlement on the St. Lawrence, inhabited mostly by Mohawk but with some Oneida, Onondaga and Cayuga people. It's worth keeping in mind that at the time of de la Chaume's visit, Pauline Johnson had just published her first full-length poem, "My Little Jean." Johnson, whose father was Mohawk and mother was English, would have had much in common with the people de la Chaume met at Caughnawaga.

41 In the winters of 1883-1885, ice palaces were erected in Dominion Square, Montreal, built of blocks of ice from the Lachine canal. The first of these ice palaces had a roof made of boughs drenched in water, frozen to make a solid, enclosed structure. The windows were formed of sheets of ice as thin as glass.

42 Ned Hanlan won the world sculling championship in England in 1880 when he beat Australian Edward Trickett by three lengths. He defended his world crown six times before losing it to Australian William Beach in 1884, the year after he came to de la Chaume's attention. Hanlan later operated a hotel founded by his father on Hanlan's Point on the Toronto Islands and eventually became an alderman of the City of Toronto. He was featured on a Canadian stamp in 1980.

43 The Rosli Hotel was located at 16 Bridge Street at the corner of Cataract Avenue. It even-tually burned and was replaced by the New Rosli House.

44 In 1875, Captain Matthew Webb was the first person to successfully swim the English Channel. He was drowned in July of 1883, when he tried to swim the Whirlpool Rapids below Niagara Falls.

[45] "The above is a footnote taken by the author from the advertising folder of the Allan Line." (H. d.l.C.)

[46] Adolphe Goupil was a leading art dealer in 19th century France. His company traded in reproductions of paintings and sculptures, with branches in Europe, Australia and America. The New York gallery was at Fifth Avenue and Twenty Second Street.

[47] In October of 1883, famed singers Victor Capoul and Christine Nilsson were in New York performing in Ambroise Thomas's opera "Mignon," which was based on Goethe's "Wilhelm."

[48] Adeline or Adelina Patti was a hugely popular opera singer of the nineteenth century. She was born in Spain of Italian parents and grew up in the Bronx. Patti made a number of recordings when she was in her sixties which, apparently, confirm that her voice at its prime must have been extraordinary.

SELECTED BIBLIOGRAPHY

Bassler, Gerhard P. *Vikings to U-Boats: The German Experience in Newfoundland and Labrador*. Montreal: McGill-Queen's University Press, 2006.

Cumberland, Stuart. *Thought-Reader's Thoughts: Being the Impressions and Confessions of Stuart Cumberland*. London: Sampson Low, Marston, Searle and Rivington, 1888. Reprint New York: Arno Press, 1975.

De la Chaume, Henri. "Excursions and Entertainments in 19th Century Newfoundland," translated by James M.F. McGrath, M.D. *The Newfoundland Quarterly*, Spring 2003, pp. 26-28.

De Valpy, Charles P. *Newfoundland: A Pictorial Record*. Canada: Longman, 1972.

Dohey, Larry. Emails to R. McGrath, Dec. 3 and Dec. 24, 2008.

Encyclopedia of Newfoundland and Labrador, St. John's, NL: Newfoundland Book Publishers, 1981.

Hatton, Joseph and M. Harvey. *Newfoundland, the Oldest British Colony: Its History, Its Present Condition, and Its Prospects in the Future*. London: Chapman and Hall, 1883.

Howley, James P. *Geography of Newfoundland: For the Use of Schools*. London. Edward Stanford, 1877.

McGrath, Antonia. *Newfoundland Photography 1849-1949*. St. John's NL: Breakwater Books, 1980.

McGrath, James M. Letter to Hon. J.R. Smallwood, July 20, 1961, included with the manuscript of "Newfoundland: The Land and It's [sic] Ladies." Centre for Newfoundland Studies, Memorial University of Newfoundland.

Mott, Henry. *Newfoundland Men*. St. John's NL: Cragg, 1894.

O'Neill, Paul. *The Oldest City*. St. John's, NL: Boulder Press, 2003.

La Pêcherie de Terreneuve: droits de la France: exposés aux assertions de l'Institut Colonial. [Quebec]: imprimerie de "L'Évènement, 1876.

Perlin, A.B. (The Wayfarer) "A Gallic Glance at Nfld." *Daily News*, January 4, 1962, p. 4.

Prowse, D.W. *A History of Newfoundland*. Portugal Cove, NL: Boulder Publications, 2002.

Report of the Council of the Royal Colonial Institute on the Newfoundland Fishery Question, November, 1875. London: Unwin, 1875.

Ritcey, Joan. Emails to R. McGrath Nov. 22, 2008.

Ryan, Shannon. Letter to R. McGrath, September 17, 1997.

Shea, Sir Ambrose. *Newfoundland, its Fisheries and General Resources In 1883*. [St. John's: Provincial Archives of Newfoundland and Labrador, 1971].

White, Mary [M.] "Emile and Henri de la Chaume: Vice-Consul and Trade Attaché Respectively for France in St. John's, Newfoundland from 1 June 1882 to 19 October 1883." *The Newfoundland Quarterly* 70.3 (1974):12-16. Centre for Newfoundland Studies, Memorial University of Newfoundland.

____. Letter to Dr. J.M. McGrath, June 30, 1970.

____. Letter to Dr. J.M. McGrath, October 15, 1970.

Wilkshire, Michael. "Guardians of the French Shore." *Newfoundland Quarterly* 102.1(2009):44-51.

PHOTO CREDITS

Cover engraving, *Canadian Illustrated News*, October 5, 1872, Archives of the RC Archdiocese of St.John's.

Henri de la Chaume, *The Newfoundland Quarterly.*

Mayac, Dordogne, birthplace of Henri de la Chaume, Dr.Michel Castillon du Perron, *The Newfoundland Quarterly.*

Abbey of Chancelade, Dorgogne, France, Centre for Newfoundland Studies.

Sketch of St. John's, March 17, 1882, by Henri de la Chaume, *The Newfoundland Quarterly.*

Sir Humphrey Gilbert, PAC/C4725.

Three Mi'kmaw women in Bay St. George, Paul-Émile Miot, Library and Archives Canada/Paul-Émile Miot/PA-202288).

Government House, St. John's, 1851, De Volpy, from a drawing by W.R. Best, W. Spriat's Litho Establishment, Exeter, England.

Sir Frederick Bowker Terrington Carter, *Encyclopedia of Newfoundland and Labrador.*

Miss Clara Fisher, O'Neill, courtesy of Boulder Publications.

Michael Francis Howley, Archdiocese of St. John's.

Caricature of Tom 'Mara by Michael Howley, Archdiocese of St. John's, Bishop Howley fond 106.12.1.

Cathedral of St. John the Baptist 1878, Archdiocese of St. John's, De Volpy, drawn by E.E.B. for *Canadian Illustrated News*, 1871.

Bishop Thomas Joseph Power, McGrath, *Newfoundland Photography 1849-1949.*

Stuart Cumberland, Swann Galleries.

Icebergs off the Harbour of St. John's, De Volpy, from sketches by J.W. Hayward for *Harper's Weekly*, 1884.

Cutting a channel in the ice...March, 1880, De Volpy, drawn by C.A. Jacob's for *Frank Leslie's Illustrated Newspaper*.

Seal hunting off the coast of Newfoundland, De Volpy, engraved by Schell and Hogan for *The Graphic*, 1881.

Caught in the ice fields of the North Atlantic, De Volpy, drawn by J.O. Davidson for *Harper's Weekly*, 1882.

Miss Lucretia Stabb, drawn by Henri de la Chaume from a photograph, *The Newfoundland Quarterly*.

View from the North Side of Quidi Vidi Lake, De Volpy, *Canadian Illustrated News* 1872.

Henry Berkeley Fitzhardinge Maxse, *Encyclopedia of Newfoundland and Labrador*.

The Colonial Building, De Volpy, from J. Ross Robertson, *Landmarks of Canada*.

Edward D'Alton Shea, *Encyclopedia of Newfoundland and Labrador*.

The French Shore 1713-1783 and The French Shore 1783-1904. *Encyclopedia of Newfoundland and Labrador*.

William Whiteway, Mott, *Newfoundland Men*.

French Rooms at St. Julian Harbour, Prowse, courtesy of Boulder Publications.

French Rooms at Cape Rouge Harbour, Prowse, Courtesy of Boulder Publications.

Guardians of a Fishing Room and his Family, Jacques Cartier Island, Prowse, courtesy of Boulder Publications.

French Fishing Boat, Prowse, courtesy of Boulder Publications.

Quidi Vidi village, McGrath, *Newfoundland Photography 1849-1949*.

The Newfoundland Cod Fisheries, De Volpy, *Canadian Illustrated News, 1871*.

Off for the Banks, De Volpy, drawn by C. Patsons for *Harper's New Monthly Magazine*, 1861.

Dr. Thomas Howley, Archives of the Roman Catholic Archdiocese of St. John's.

The Railway Station at Fort William, *Encyclopedia of Newfoundland and Labrador.*

Holyrood, *Encyclopedia of Newfoundland and Labrador.*

Father John St. John, Archives of the Roman Catholic Archdiocese of St. John's.

Salmonier Church, Prowse, photo by Parsons, courtesy of Boulder Publications.

Mother Mary Magdalen O'Shaughnessy, Archives of the Roman Catholic Archdiocese of St. John's.

Presentation Convent, *Encyclopedia of Newfoundland and Labrador.*

Admiral John Edward Commerell, *Vanity Fair.*

Robert Henry Prowse, Mott, *Newfoundland Men.*

Caughnawaga, Quebec, Collegial Centre for Educational Materials Development, Wikipedia.

Ice Castles at Montreal, Victoriana.com.

Ned Hanlan, Osprey Oars, ospreyors.com <http://ospreyors.com>.

The Rosli Hotel, Bridge Street, Niagara Falls, Niagara Falls Public Library.

Captain Matthew Webb, Niagara Falls Public Library.

Adelina Patti, *entertainment.webshots.com.*

BIOGRAPHIES

HENRI DE LA CHAUME (1861-1949) served as trade attache to the French Vice-Consul at St. John's from 1882-3. His book about that time, *Terre-Neuve et les Terre-Neuviennes*, was published the year after his return to France. A gifted artist and horticulturalist, de la Chaume lived for many years at the Abbey of Chancelade, Dordogne, where he was the organist.

DR. J.M.F. MCGRATH, (1902-1975) a native Newfoundlander, was a graduate of the National University of Ireland. After many years as a district medical officer, he specialized in Public Health and was appointed Minister of Health for Newfoundland from 1956 to 1967. He also served in the Finance portfolio. An avid bibliophile, McGrath was the author of a volume of poetry and numerous occasional pieces.

ROBIN MCGRATH (1949-) earned a PhD from the University of Western Ontario and taught Aboriginal and Early Canadian Literature as an Associate Professor at the University of Alberta. She is the author or editor of almost two dozen books, her most recent being a novel, *The Winterhouse*. McGrath is the winner of the inaugural Newfoudland and Labrador Heritage and History Award for literature.